HALAKHAH and POLITICS

THE LIBRARY OF JEWISH LAW AND ETHICS
VOLUME XIV
EDITED BY NORMAN LAMM
President and Jakob and Erna Michael professor of Jewish philosophy
Yeshiva University

HALAKHAH and POLITICS

The Jewish Idea of the State

By

SOL ROTH

KTAV PUBLISHING HOUSE, INC.
YESHIVA UNIVERSITY PRESS
NEW YORK AND HOBOKEN

Library of Congress Cataloging-in-Publication Data
Roth, Sol.
  Halakhah and politics: the Jewish idea of the state/by Sol
Roth.

     p.   cm. — (Library of Jewish law and ethics; v. 14)
  Bibliography: p.
  Includes index.
  ISBN 0-88125-129-1
  1. Politics in rabbinical literature. 2. Judaism and state.
3. Judaism and politics. 4. Jewish law. I. Title. II. Series.
BM496.9.P64R68 1988
296.3'877—dc19   87-35250
                                       CIP

MANUFACTURED IN THE UNITED STATES OF AMERICA

To My Parents
Joseph Roth
יוסף יהושע בן שלום
and
Miriam Roth
מרים בת יהושע
who
more than anyone else
shaped my heart and my mind
Their Memory is a Blessing

Table of Contents

Editor's Foreword

A quick glance at the chapter headings of this volume reveals both the variety of topics treated and the thematic cohesiveness of the book as a whole.

Rabbi Roth — the Samson Raphael Hirsch Professor of Torah im Derekh Eretz at Yeshiva University and Rabbi of the Fifth Avenue Synagogue in New York City — integrates the vision of the Jewish tradition with the operating concepts of Western political philosophy in order to illuminate some of the central problems in political life from the vantage of Halakhah, Agadah, and the exegetical heritage of Judaism.

There is hardly a more compelling theme to capture the attention of a scholar of Dr. Roth's competence and his standing as an exemplar of the marvelous mastery of both worlds, that of Judaism and that of general, secular culture.

NORMAN LAMM

Preface

This volume is an application of the ideal of *Torah im Derekh Eretz* to the domain of political theory. Its fundamental standpoint is that of the *Halakhah* whose principles are elaborated here in a manner that preserves their authenticity. They are formulated, however, in the terminology of contemporary political discourse whose ideas serve to relate *Halakhah* to contemporary experience. The result is the incorporation into Torah of concepts and methodology that are associated with disciplines which are normally perceived as belonging to the realm of general culture.

It is part of the *Torah im Derekh Eretz* ideal that we relate in a very positive way to the society in which we find ourselves. For Samson R. Hirsch, the author of the *Torah im Derekh Eretz* philosophy, this meant the celebration of Emancipation; that is, the joyful acceptance of citizenship and equality in the countries to which we belong. Many leading sages greeted this state of affairs as a dubious blessing. They believed that the preservation of Judaism required the kind of separation from gentile communities that precludes political equality. The advocates of the Hirsch ideal, on the other hand, perceived Emancipation as a unadulterated blessing, welcomed it with enthusiasm, and looked forward to a life unhampered by the liabilities of injustice and persecution.

The adoption of the Hirsch posture in our own day and in our own society implies, indeed necessitates, that we clarify the political conceptions of Judaism as well as those of democracy. Their respective ideas ought not to be confused, and even while they differ in some ways because they address different types of political contexts, the ideas emerging out of the theory of democracy can and should be incorporated into the life of the Torah community. The American political system is one variety of *derekh eretz* that needs to be brought into relation with Torah.

It is the author's hope, by means of this book, to contribute to the achievement of this goal.

At this time, I should like to acknowledge, with a great deal of gratitude the encouragement that I have received from Jacques and Hanna Schwalbe, who have dedicated themselves with an impressive degree of success to the propogation of the philosophy of Samson R. Hirsch, to focus in my own literary efforts on Hirsch's concept of *Torah im Derekh Eretz*. It has been a rewarding undertaking. My appreciation to Dr. Norman Lamm, President of Yeshiva University and editor of the *Library of Jewish Law and Ethics* for inviting me to write this volume for the Series.

SOL ROTH
Samson R. Hirsch Professor of Torah
and Derekh Eretz of Yeshiva University

Acknowledgements

The chapter entitled "Power" appeared in the *Rabbi Joseph H. Look-stein Memorial Volume* published by KTAV Publishing House, Inc. in 1980 under the heading, "The Dilemma of Power."

The chapter, "Land," first appeared in the Fall 1977 issue of *Tradition* with the title, "The Right to the Land."

The chapter, "Sovereignty," appeared in the 1977-1978 issue of *Gesher* under the heading, "Political Sovereignty: A Jewish View."

The chapter, "Freedom," first appeared in the Fall 1972 issue of *Tradition* with the title "Two Concepts of Freedom."

The chapter entitled "Peace" appeared in *Tradition and Transition: Essays Presented to Chief Rabbi Sir Immanuel Jakobovits* published by Jews' College in 1986 under the heading "Peace as a Political Value."

The chapter, "Social Policy," appeared in *Formation of Social Policy in the Catholic and Jewish Traditions* published by University of Notre Dame Press in 1980 and was entitled, "Methodology and Social Policy: A Jewish Perspective."

The chapter, "Revolution," appeared in the Fall 1971 issue of *Judaism* with the title "The Morality of Revolution: A Jewish View."

All but three of these chapters were written explicitly for this book and were contributed on invitation to various publications. The three chapters which were prompted by other considerations required only minor modification to justify their incorporation into a volume that lays claim to thematic unity.

Introduction

Halakhah and Politics: The Jewish Idea of the State is a companion to my volume entitled *The Jewish Idea of Community*. Both represent an attempt to contribute to Jewish social philosophy—an area of philosophic activity that has been largely neglected in the course of the history of Jewish thought. Indeed, political philosophy elicited even less interest than the philosophy of community because, while Jewish communities existed throughout the period of exile, and the concepts inherent in the idea of community called for clarification, a Jewish state was perceived until modern times as an unattainable dream. Philosophic reflection is much more likely when related to contemporary issues.

It is evident that the idea of a state differs from that of a community; indeed, it does so in a variety of ways. A comparison of the two will reveal the concepts that need to be analyzed in the development of the political component of Judaism's social philosophy.

For the sake of clarity, it should be noted that the word *community* will be employed here to refer, not to a geographic community, but to a community of commitment. The difference between the two is clear. A geographic community is most often pluralistic; at least in a democratic society, it generally encompasses a variety of groups who practice diverse creeds and adhere to conflicting ideologies. A community of commitment is homogeneous; each of its members adopts the identical creed, though the degree of observance may vary among them.

1

Fundamental to the existence of a community is the exemplification of certain *attitudes* by its citizens; basic to the existence of a state is the exercise of *power* by those who govern. The community focus is primarily the cultivation of internal commitment to values by which the community defines itself. It may employ force and persuasion to accomplish its purpose—the rod in the classroom and ostracism in the public domain, for example—but its essential goal is the development of attitudes, the inculcation of commitment. It seeks to motivate and to inspire its members to adopt a common creed in order to assure the community's cohesiveness and preservation. The state, on the other hand, relies primarily on power—indeed it is an instrument of power, and it is so labeled in the international forum of states—to achieve the values that it seeks to embody in social patterns of conduct. This is not to say that the state does not strive to instill commitment to values as well; what is intended, rather, is that the state does not rely on voluntary obedience to rules that reflect these values, but seeks to enforce them.

The attitudes on which the preservation of the Jewish community ultimately depends, according to religious, traditional-minded Jews, are a feeling of cultural distinction, a sense of common destiny, the experience of mutual love, a belief in a covenantal commitment, and so forth. The existence of a state, on the other hand, depends on the exercise of power by a central authority. The power of the state is utilized, first, to protect the community from any threats that may be mounted from sources external to it and, second, to preserve the kind of order which will make it possible for the community to live in peace and to engage in the struggle to realize the values to which it is committed.

Accordingly, both state and community are concerned with the realization of value—but their respective thrusts differ. The primary values that a state wishes to achieve differ from those aimed at by a community. This is particularly the case in a pluralistic democratic society. In such a political context, while government pursues freedom, equality, and justice, and substantially focuses on related activities, a community within such a society will aspire as well to a whole series of other values. In the case of the Jewish community, these values—the study of Torah and a relation with God, for instance—are biblically prescribed and are irrelevant to a democratic polity. In a homogeneous nonpluralistic state, on the other hand, it is possible for the government to involve itself in legislation to enforce values that are unique to a culture as well. This would be the case if, for example, the Jewish state were theocratic in nature. Even so, however, the state would still differ from a community in that while the latter's focus is the unique cultural values that distinguish it from other communities, the state seeks primarily to enforce those that are universal, such as equality, justice, and peace.

In the religious context of Judaism, this distinction may be expressed by saying that while the community is concerned with values associated with the category of *kedushah*, the sacred, the state concentrates on those that derive from *malkhut*, sovereignty. The achievement of sanctity requires the appropriation of values that have as their ultimate end a relationship with the Divine Being, while the thrust of sovereignty is the exemplification of values that will assure justice in human relations and the defense of the community against external threats. This is the case even while, in a homogeneous society, the ruling authority may strive to create conditions which will allow and facilitate the pursuit of values that are rooted in the sacred. The *navi*, the prophet, and the *melekh*, the king, in the ancient homogeneous Jewish society, were indeed directed towards the same ultimate goal; their immediate purposes, however, differed. The prophet stuggled to enhance the Jew's awareness of God's presence and the obligations deriving from that awareness, while the objective of the king was essentially terrestrial in character, that is, the protection of the community and justice in human relations.

The aim of this book is the theoretical exploration of the values that inhere in the Jewish idea of a state. It is clear that there is value in power. Though it needs to be restrained, power is indispensable to the existence of a state. The Jewish concept of power must, therefore, receive elaboration at the start, and this will indeed be the theme of the first chapter.

A state presupposes the existence of a stretch of land on which its citizens reside. A government in exile is a political entity with which existing states must deal because of the threat it represents, but it does not constitute a state. Nevertheless, the concept of land is not often included in political analysis. It must, however, be incorporated into a development of the Jewish idea of a state because of the unique role which land occupies in Jewish political thought.

The notion of sovereignty in Jewish religious thought is complicated by the circumstance that the ruling authority is not autonomous. To some extent, it must subordinate itself to the divine will. Because of the tension that may very well arise between the exercise of human power and divine authority, there were some who frowned on the institution of sovereignty altogether. The questions of the legitimacy of sovereignty and the controlling parameters applicable to it must be addressed.

A central theme in all political discussion is justice. While, in truth, every part of the idea of a state somehow relates to justice and, accordingly, questions such as the use of power, the right to land, and the exercise of sovereignty (the themes of the three initial chapters) can also be subsumed under this general rubric, the idea of justice is often more narrowly construed.

One value that is intimately associated with the idea of justice is that of equality. It is generally held that a just society is one in which citizens are treated equally. This claim too raises important questions. How is this concept to be understood? Is the equality of all citizens in a state a realizable goal?

Further, to what extent is the consent of the governed essential to assure that a piece of legislation is just, and what really constitues consent? In addition, is dissent permissible in a just society?

Freedom, it is currently granted, is also an essential component of justice. Associated with the notion of freedom are the concepts of individualism and human rights. These vague and ambiguous ideas also require analysis. It is often suggested that the Jewish concept of freedom is identical with its American counterpart. The suggestion is clearly false. What then is the Jewish concept of freedom? Does Judaism share democracy's interpretation of the idea of individualism, namely, that everyone has the right to do as he wishes? Clearly not! What then is the Jewish view on individualism? Does Judaism accept the notion of human rights? The question becomes striking when it is noticed that Judaism does not often speak of the rights of man but of his obligations.

What role does the principle of the majority play in Jewish political theory? While this principle is at the foundation of a democratic society, it should be remembered that religious Judaism advocates a polity that is more in the nature of a theocracy than a democracy. Is there any room in Judaism for the majority principle as a political instrument?

Each of these questions focuses on an aspect of the general principle of political justice, and to each a chapter will be devoted.

The volume includes still other themes that are relevant to political discussion. Peace is a political objective, but how is it to be rated in comparison with justice, that is, which is to be assigned priority?

The Jewish people lived in exile for two millennia. Does such a condition have political implications?

It is the responsibility of government to effect transformations when existing social conditions are found to be painful and frustrating to citizens. Under such circumstances, what is the nature of the changes that should be undertaken? If the government fails to act, may the people engage in revolution?

These are the questions addressed in this volume. Its purpose is to clarify the distinguishing features of Jewish political thought, to contrast Jewish approaches with those that we generally associate with democracy, and to gain an understanding of the contribution that religious-minded Jews would make to the political evolution of the Jewish state.

1

Power

It is a common view that Judaism's response to power is one of negation and rejection. A noted contemporary Jewish historian wrote, "The exaltation of powerlessness in the Jewish religion found its counterpart in the evolution of a people without political power."[1] This suggests that the Jewish denigration of power is a matter of both principle and fact. Powerlessness is, on the one hand, an ideal (it is exalted), and on the other, it is a character of the life of the Jewish people. It is a trait of Jewish history.

The domain of power that was most obviously denied to Jews during the last two millennia and until recently is the political. The creation of the modern State of Israel represents the restoration to the Jew of this as well as other forms of power, for example, military. Shall he feel uncomfortable because of these acquisitions? Is power a curse, or is it, perhaps, a blessing?

Certain forms of power contain within themselves the seeds of both good and evil. The very same variety of power is often valuable and a threat. Shall it be appropriated because of its utility, or shall it be rejected because of its capacity to injure? This indeed is the dilemma of power. It is the purpose of this chapter to clarify this dilemma and to indicate how it is resolved in the context of Jewish thought.

7

I

Power, in the sense in which this term is applied to man, may be defined as the ability to realize ends.[2] A variety of means are available to man for the attainment of his purposes. They include inherent capacities, such as intelligence, speech, knowledge, and determination; objects to which men are generally responsive, such as weapons, political authority, and money; natural forces, such as electricity and magnetism, etc. These things, however, are not in themselves powers, because power is not a character of things but of individuals who utilize such things as means.

A natural force, for example, is not a power. When an object exerts a force, it functions as a cause, not as a means; the result of its action is the production of an effect, not the attainment of an objective. Force is a causal notion; power is purposive. The force of gravity causes the apple, when its connection to the tree grows weak, to fall; a bolt of lightning, an electrical force, is the cause of the fire in the house. In neither case is there a question of realizing a goal. It is otherwise with power. When we learn to control the force of electricity and we utilize it to the end, for example, of illuminating our homes, it becomes a means, and the one to whom it is available possesses power.

There are other forms of power. The possession of money, the means for acquiring things one needs or wants, confers upon an individual economic power. If knowledge is translatable into technology, then, as Francis Bacon maintained, it is a power.[3] Intellectual capacity and determination, essential components in the process of achieving objectives that require intelligence as well as the prolonged and consistent expenditure of effort, are elements of mental power. In brief, man has power when such things as mental capacities, talents, attitudes, objects, and natural forces are available to him to use as means.

An important conclusion may be drawn immediately. In view of the fact that human purposes generally require power for their attainment, power cannot be intrinsically evil. Every human enterprise involves the use of power. According to the Jewish conception, *work* is to be defined as creative activity in the material domain.[4] The creative act generally requires the use of means.

Whether the creative goal is a crop, a garment, a house, a painting, or a literary work; muscle, talent, and determination, at the very least, are essential. To create, therefore, is to use power. Power cannot then be rejected altogether. It cannot be identified as inherently evil.

Power is, however, subject to moral judgment. In this sense, it is again to be distinguished from force. Force is neutral and amoral—it can be described as blind, strong, explosive, etc., but not as evil. From the human perspective, at least, the force of gravity is neither good nor bad; it is merely there, a fact of life which must be acknowledged and taken into account. Power, on the other hand, can be good or evil—though not in an intrinsic but in a derived sense. It acquires its moral character, not from some trait of that which is used as a means, but from the purpose it serves.

We may proceed to the description of the circumstances that prompt us to suspect and sometimes to reject power. Power may justly be challenged on moral grounds in a variety of circumstances: (1) when it is used for an immoral purpose; (2) when too much of it is concentrated in the hands of a single individual; (3) when it becomes a purpose in itself.

1. When the ability that constitutes power is applied in violation of a moral precept, it is evil in use. Even knowledge, the possession of which is generally lauded, becomes evil when its translation into technology serves the purpose of genocide. But it is clear that what, in this instance, is evil is not the power but the manner of its use. The very same power may be applied towards the attainment of a noble aim.

2. When too much power is concentrated in the hands of a single individual, it may, from the standpoint of morality or religion, have a detrimental impact on personality. The Bible, in one of its passages, offers an estimate of the probable consequences of excessive economic power.

Lest when thou hast eaten and are full, and hast built goodly homes, and dwelt therein; and when thy herds and thy flocks multiply, and thy silver and thy gold is multiplied, and all that

thou hast is multiplied; then thine heart be lifted up, and thou
forget the Lord thy God, which brought thee out of the land
of Egypt, from the house of bondage.[5]

A demand to limit the accumulation of economic power is also
made, and probably for the same reason, in the case of the sovereign. The Bible declares:

> But he shall not multiply horses to himself . . . neither shall
> he multiply wives to himself . . . neither shall he greatly mul-
> tiply to himself silver and gold.[6]

It is apparently the biblical view that the possession of excessive
power may have, as a consequence, the rejection of God.

Indeed, the religious attitude cannot coexist with the exaggerated sense of power which, in fact, often accompanies its acquisition in large quantities. Jewish thinkers have maintained that
the essential religious virtue, without which the genuine religious
experience is impossible, is the sense of humility.[7] But this sense
is incompatible with an exaggerated feeling of power. One claim
that the truly religious personality must, according to biblical prescription, studiously avoid is, "My power and the might of mine
hand hath gotten me this wealth,"[8] for such a declaration entails
the denial that the Divine Being has a role in the affairs of men.
The sovereign and the wealthy man are particularly vulnerable
to such arrogance. It is important to note that so is the man of
knowledge. Many believe that, because of the power at his disposal, made available by the advance in scientific technology, there
is no obstacle in the path of human progress that man cannot, by
his knowledge and ingenuity, overcome. The implication is that
man does not need a Higher Being. It is well known that the
growth of science has been accompanied by a concomitant decline
in religion. This has resulted, not so much from the fact that it
is possible to interpret the claims of science as contradicting those
of religion, as from the fact that the sense of power, generated
by the possession of scientific knowledge, is incompatible with the
sense of humility that is a prerequisite to the religious experience.

If it were the case that an individual could estimate correctly what he could achieve with the power placed at his disposal, that is, if his sense of power were not exaggerated, his possession of it would probably not be as damaging as, in fact, it is. But power is deceptive. Men and nations are often deluded by it into believing that they can control their own destinies as well as the fate of others. Economic and military power conveys this feeling; science does it as well. But the *sense* of power does not always coincide with its *reality*. Man frequently believes that he can do more than his power will actually allow. Such exaggeration is exhibited in a series of judgments which have or, at least, have had popular acceptance. One of these declares that there is nothing that money cannot buy. It is well known that this judgment is false—money cannot, in many instances, purchase good health or long life. Another has it that military victory depends on getting there first with the most. This too is false—the military strategy of Egypt and Syria during the Yom Kippur War was an attempt at applying this principle, but had the United States not intervened, the Arabs would have sustained a disastrous defeat. It was similar exaggeration that inspired the optimistic sentiment which claimed, for science, the capacity to solve all human problems and to realize the conditions of a utopia.[9] The dream, however, is false; its vision is unrealizable. Knowledge does not have such potency. Science can also bring about the destruction of mankind.

3. But power has still another consequence that is incompatible with morality, namely, it is itself sometimes turned into an end. That which was originally intended as a means to acceptable and humane objectives sometimes becomes an ultimate purpose. J. S. Mill supplies one illustration of this fact. Money, originally a means for the acquisition of material goods, is frequently pursued for its own sake.[10] When such a transformation occurs, it can be damaging.

Hence, the Jewish sovereign was required to carry a Torah and to read it with regularity so that he would always subordinate the power of the prince to Torah ideals and never permit that power itself to become the ideal.

And it shall be, when he sitteth on the throne of his kingdom, that he shall write him a copy of this law in a book. . . . And it shall be with him, and he shall read therein all the days of his life; that he may learn to fear the Lord his God, to keep all the words of this law and these statutes, to do them; that his heart shall not be lifted up above his brethren, and that he turn not aside from the commandment, to the right hand or to the left.[11]

What are the consequences of turning power into the ultimate purpose of life? It intensifies egoism, stifles compassion, and makes the one who is committed to its accumulation indifferent to the pain and anguish of his fellow man. If power is regarded as a means, then it acquires a moral character if the purpose for which it is used is moral. If treated as an end, and all other purposes are subordinated to it, it ceases to have positive moral value and, to the contrary, becomes an evil—for then the controlling aim of the one who perseveres to acquire it is to amass for himself a great deal of whatever form of power he chooses. In his quest for this, his highest purpose, he will be insensitive to the needs of others, exploit them when necessary to realize his objective, and permit himself to afflict them with acts of cruelty.

The logical consequences of the view that makes the acquisition of power ultimate were drawn by Nietzsche, who advocated a form of life that is characterized by the "will to power." He writes:

It cannot be helped: the sentiment of surrender, of sacrifice for one's neighbor, and all self-renunciation morality, must be mercilessly called to account, and brought to judgment. . . . There is far too much witchery and sugar in the sentiments "for others" and "not for myself" for one not needing to be doubly distrustful here, and for one asking promptly: "Are they not perhaps—deceptions?"[12]

It is unnecessary to press the point. History testifies endlessly how men and nations who lusted for power and achieved it spread death and bloodshed with reckless abandon among vanquished and innocent victims. Power, treated as an end in itself, dehumanizes; it often reduces man to the condition of the beast.

In sum, while power is not intrinsically bad, it may be the cause of a great deal of harm: it may be used to achieve a purpose that is inherently evil; a massive accumulation of it may—though it need not—have damaging effects on personality; turned by man into a final purpose it will, in all likelihood, make him insensitive and cruel. Given the enormously damaging potential of certain forms of power—in the military and political spheres, for instance—some may be prompted to repudiate these varieties of power altogether. This is one side of our dilemma.

II

The other side emerges out of the consideration that even those forms of power that are potentially harmful are, in other circumstances, useful and beneficial. Of course, the value of power employed for the realization of a personal objective when that use does not impinge upon another human being is rarely doubtful. It is, for example, morally right, and obviously so, to work for the sake of earning a livelihood, to study in order to accumulate knowledge, and to apply it to one's advantage. The challenge to the legitimacy of power emerges, with force, when power is applied to injure other human beings or to influence them to follow a certain course of action. Under what conditions, if any, is it morally right to do so?

It should be noted, at the start, that there are two ways of compelling another—one is the way of the book, and the other that of the sword. Now, the proverbial struggle between the book and the sword is not an antagonism between something other than power and power. It is, in fact, an opposition between two forms of power. One communicates; the other destroys or threatens to do so. One uses the method of persuasion; the other that of coercion. The attempt to persuade is directed at volition, while the attempt to coerce is directed at action. When an individual is persuaded, he acts in conformity to his will; when he is coerced, he acts contrary to his will. What, now, are the methods of persuasion, the powers symbolized by the book, and the methods of coercion, the powers represented by the sword?

We will start with the book. The book symbolizes, in the first place, the power of technology. Such power may be used for a variety of purposes; one of these is to exercise control over the thought and actions of others. One may, after all, persuade another by psychological and social techniques, propaganda, for example, as well as by logical argument or emotional appeal. The modern miracle, the television set, is a striking example of the way technology aids man in molding the thinking and directing the behavior of others.

The book, however, also symbolizes cultural power. This form of power belongs to a people whose culture gives it the capacity to achieve its social aims and to prevail on those beyond its boundaries to adopt its cultural patterns. One people's cultural power is greater than another's when it is able to emerge successfully from a cultural collision where the value systems embedded in the two cultures are incompatible. A people may be militarily weak but culturally strong. The ancient empires of Greece and Rome were destroyed, but their values survived. Those classic cultures are still reflected in contemporary Western civilization. From a military standpoint, the Jewish people could not have had less strength during the past two thousand years, but it had the cultural power to preserve its way of life and to exert influence on others. It is well known that the vanquished on the field of battle are frequently victorious in the cultural struggle. This is the result of cultural power.

Such power is derived from two factors: one is the inherent vitality of the culture in question, and the second is the sense of commitment of those who identify with it. A culture, because of its intrinsic character, and even without any deliberate effort on the part of its adherents to impose it, will influence human action and patterns of social conduct. The Torah, to the religious Jewish mind, supplies just this kind of power to the Jew. The prayer book, in a passage recited immediately before the Torah is returned to the ark, puts it as follows:

I give you good instruction, forsake not my Torah. It is a tree of life to those who take hold of it, and happy are those who support it. Its ways are ways of pleasantness and all its paths are peace.

Torah, because of its inherent character, is declared to be an effective means to the achievement of individual as well as social aims.

The second component of cultural power is commitment.[13] It consists in the capacity to adhere to a pattern of behavior required by an adopted creed no matter what the obstacles along the way. It is such uncompromising resolution that enables the committed Jew to exert influence on his own community, and to assure the preservation of Jewish life.

Two forms of power are, therefore, symbolized by the book; one is technological, and the other cultural. Cultural power, in turn, divides into two components—the inherent quality of the culture and commitment. However, when one speaks of the power of the book possessed by the people of the book, it is only cultural power that is intended. The Bible provides few technological clues; but it does express a system of values that makes available a variety of satisfactions, and it does inspire a sense of commitment that makes possible the preservation of Judaism even in the condition of exile and diaspora.[14]

The sword has two symbolic meanings. In a wider sense, it represents any form of coercion other than persuasion by argument, emotional appeal, or psychological techniques. It includes punitive methods, such as incarceration and fines. In a narrower application, the sword symbolizes acts of violence that result in pain and death. It is clear that Judaism permits the use of the sword, even in its narrower sense, in a variety of circumstances.

One of these is the courts. Judges are allowed to use instruments of coercion, represented by the rod, to compel compliance with their decisions.[15] They are authorized to inflict the death penalty as well. When Rabbis Tarfon and Akiva declared that, had they served in the Sanhedrin, the death penalty would never have been carried out, Rabbi Shimon ben Gamaliel responded that their policy would have led to an increase in the number of murderers among Jews.[16] This rabbinic debate, however, does not deal with the question whether the court's use of violence is justified by moral standards. Such a procedure is clearly held to be moral—it is, after all, biblically prescribed. A method that is intrinsically immoral could not have received such sanction. The dispute could be interpreted as focusing on the question whether it is necesssary to apply the biblical precept to impose the death penalty in order to achieve the Bible's objectives. There are other biblical precepts—that dealing with the rebellious son, for example—which according to rabbinic interpretation were enunciated for pedagogic reasons, not for the sake of implementation.[17] In any case, Maimonides declares as a matter of law that while a court that imposes the death penalty more than once in seven years is called a murderous court, when circumstances and law require it, this penalty should be imposed with frequency.[18] On the Jewish view, therefore, violence may be practiced, with legitimacy, in the courtroom.

It may also be used in war. Biblical and rabbinic passages endorsing and even urging military confrontation are too numerous to require a demonstration of the claim that violence in war is compatible with the Jewish moral conscience. There *is* such a thing as a justifiable war.

The sword should, of course, be applied with restraint. In the case of the *rodef*, for example, that is, one who is pursuing another with the intent to kill, an act of violence to prevent the murder is required. Nevertheless, if it is possible to prevent the killing by merely maiming the assailant, it is not permitted to take his life.[19] Even an act of violence does not justify a similar act equal and opposite. Violence is allowed, if it is needed, to prevent the crime, but death may be inflicted in the process only if there is no alternative course of action.

Neither should violence be employed in society if the social objective can be achieved in some other way. I argue below that the use of violence to effect a social transformation is not justified on the Jewish view.[20] Judaism does not endorse the modern ideology of revolution, which calls for the use of violence as a means of effecting changes of an economic and political variety. Certainly the prophets, preoccupied though they were with questions of social justice, engaged in exhortation and demonstration to achieve social progress, but they did not resort to the use of violence.

But violence is essential in the case of war. Judaism does not accept the theory of pacifism, which rejects the use of the sword under any conditions. This theory is based on either of two considerations. (1) Violence is inherently evil; it cannot be regarded as merely a means which shares in the moral character of the end that it serves. Its moral quality, on this view, is independent of any subsidiary considerations—it is intrinsically immoral. (2) Violence may never be employed, because any social end to which it may be regarded as an instrument can be attained by other means. Bertrand Russell, for example, expounded the second view in an essay in which he advocated the use of passive resistance.[21] He argued that even in the extreme, when a country is faced with aggression, if violence is not met with violence, the citizens of the attacking country will oppose their government's policy and bring the invasion to an end; and that, in any case, soldiers will not raise the sword against those who offer no resistance because there is no victory or glory to be gained. The positive objectives of the society under attack can subsequently be attained through a policy of passive resistance.

Judaism, however, rejects both bases for pacifism. It denies that the sword is inherently evil; it claims further that there are circumstances in which the powers symbolized by the book are not adequate to the goal of physical and cultural self-preservation. The Holocaust, of course, is one glaring counterexample to Russell's thesis that passivity brings an end to bloodshed. It may even be regarded as evidence for the contrary hypothesis, namely, men become more bloodthirsty when their victims offer little resistance.

III

Judaism's affirmation of power is expressed in many ways; one of these is its endorsement of the institution of the state. When the Bible declares "Thou shalt set a king over thee,"[22] two things are apparently intended. One is the creation of a state, that is, a government; the second is that the form of government shall be a monarchy. Setting aside, for the present, the second component of this commandment, it is evident that the Bible requires the establishment of a state.

The state is an instrument for the achievement of primarily social objectives. These objectives may be interpreted in ideal terms. The purpose of the state could be construed, for example, as that of preserving freedom, of assuring the equitable distribution of goods, or of guaranteeing that the public patterns of behavior shall reflect a certain system of values. Its objectives may also be construed in empirical terms. One may argue that whatever the declared goals of a government may be, a state is really an instrument of oppression of the ruled by those who rule. In all cases, however, whether we are contemplating a democratic, monarchial, or totalitarian government, the state, most fundamentally, is an instrument for the achievement of ends in a social context.

The state is, then, a source of power. Its power derives from the organization of other sources of power available to it—economic, military, technological, cultural, etc. Since its power is, to some extent, proportional to the quantities of the various concentrations of power which it administers, the state is a *vast* source of power.

The determination by an exiled people to restore its state is then, basically, a repudiation of powerlessness and an attempt to regain the kind of power which would enable it to achieve large and historic objectives. This applies particularly to the enterprise of Zionism. Forms of Zionism may be distinguished by their differing objectives. One sought a state as a means of eliminating anti-Semitism; another held it to be essential to cultural development; a third believed it to be necessary for the attainment of religious goals. But what all Zionists sought fundamentally was the restoration of a source of power that was a prerequisite to the transformation of Jewish life.

In this regard, the Jewish religion is to be distinguished from others. Judaism does not essentially oppose temporal power to divine power. The city of man is not necessarily antagonistic to the city of God; the human city is rather a matrix in which divine precepts may be translated into action. Judaism does not formulate a conception of religion which is limited, in its concerns, to man's relations with his fellow man and God. It also introduces

the idea of a state in which the power that it makes available may
be utilized to realize, in individual conduct and social action, the
values of Jewish life.

IV

Judaism's affirmation of power is also manifest in its inclusion of
the element of power in its conception of three central social
ideals, namely, freedom, justice, and peace.

Power is an essential component in the Jewish idea of freedom.
The free personality is not the one who has the *right* to do as *he
wishes*, but the one who has the *power* to do as *he should*. The
achievement of freedom for the Jew is associated with an historic
event, the exodus from Egypt; not with a pronouncement, com-
munally agreed upon, similar to the American Declaration of Independence, or a contractual agreement such as a constitution.
What the Hebrew people acquired upon its departure from Egypt,
therefore, was not a right, but the power to do that which it could
not do in a condition of slavery.

Hence, the Jewish conception of freedom differs significantly
from the American. To the American, freedom is primarily a
right. It is also a power but only to the extent that a right is
meaningless unless it is accompanied by the power to exercise the
right. Of what value, for example, is the right to be elected president of the United States if one's position in society renders it
impossible to take advantage of the right? For Judaism, however,
freedom is not a right, but a power.

It is for this reason that Judaism conceives of freedom as something capable of growing and expanding. The departure from
slavery is merely one step in the direction of freedom. The rabbis
add, "One is not free unless he studies the Torah."[23] To the extent
that study adds to human power, it augments freedom. The establishment of a state is still another move towards freedom because a state makes available an enormous reservoir of power.
This, I believe, is the meaning of the passage in the first paragraph
of the Passover Haggadah which declares, "This year we are here,
next year we shall be in the land of Israel; this year we are slaves.

next year we shall be free." Life in the Jewish state is thus associated with the ideal of freedom. The Jewish state may or may
not make available to the Jew certain rights that he did not enjoy
in other countries; but it certainly grants him, in abundance, the
kind of power that he lacked elsewhere. Hence, the Jewish state
represents a development in Jewish freedom.

Power is also associated, in an essential way, with the dominion
of justice. However one may define this concept, it remains the
Jewish view that he whose behavior conforms to the requirements
of justice should be rewarded, while he whose conduct violates
them should be punished. Now reward and punishment, on the
Jewish view, are not natural, but imposed consequences. The rewards of moral action do not flow from it in the manner in which
an effect follows from a cause. Good health or prosperity are not
held to result, *in a natural way*, from the act of honesty or philanthropy. If they did, we would not need to confront the talmudic
dilemma of "the righteous who suffer and the wicked who pros-
per."[24] Painful consequences of unjust behavior must be imposed
by some authority that has the power to do so and that is external
to the natural course of events. It involves a deliberate decision
and the application of available power.

Peace too requires power to preserve it. The rabbis urge us to
"pray for the peace of the government; for were it not for the
fear of it, men would swallow each other alive."[25] Peace, in the
normal conditions of human society, depends on the respect for
its authority that a political power can impose upon its citizenry.
Without such power, the natural state would be, as Hobbes also
maintained, one of war of every man against every man. It is
interesting to note that, on the rabbinic view, power will be needed
to bring about the peace of the messianic era as well. According
to Maimonides, the chief aim of the messianic personality is to
bring the gift of peace to mankind. The nature of things will not
change in the end of days; the conditions of peace will not result
from some supernatural act of divine intervention. It will come
with the application of extraordinary power on the part of the
messianic personality, who "will compel all Israel to walk in the
path of Torah" and will fight the "battles of God" as well as the
"wars of Gog and Magog."[26]

V

Here then is the dilemma of power. On the one hand, power is essential to the achievement of human objectives. Power is indispensable even in its most massive form, namely, the state. But, on the other hand, power grown large can explode beyond moral boundaries and humane limits. When massive power is unrestrained, when its accumulation becomes an end in itself, it can be enormously detrimental. We cannot do without power, on the one hand; we must beware of it on the other. If power is to be contained within moral bounds, it must somehow be limited. How can this be done?

There are several ways of doing so. First, political power must be opposed by political power. Judaism accordingly invested the prophet with a political function. The prophet was that individual in ancient Jewish society who, in matters of social concern, stood in opposition to the king. Nathan challenged King David, and Elijah threw down the gauntlet to King Ahab. The prophet, though deprived of the panoply of physical power, exerted, by the sheer force of charisma, sufficient power to restrain even a king. The monarchial period of Jewish history was one in which there was an ongoing struggle between king and prophet—one happy consequence of which was the limitation of the power of the king. This was an external restraint on political power.

It was the very same principle that found expression in the Jewish law that made the head of state subject to the judgment of the Sanhedrin. The king could be charged in the courtroom with a violation of the law, and sentence could be imposed. This procedure was accepted without interruption with respect to the monarchs of the ancient kingdom of Judea; it was practiced up to a point with respect to the kings of Israel.[27]

This principle of opposing power with power finds application, in the context of democracy, in the principle of the separation of powers. If legislative, executive, and judicial powers are located in different institutions and controlled by different personalities, it frequently occurs that the power of one of these finds itself in a state of tension with the powers of others.

The second method of limiting power is that of distribution. The prophet Samuel was distressed when his people demanded that he designate a king to govern them. Rabbinic commentators found it difficult to justify his inclination to deny the request in the light of the biblical commandment which requires the appointment of a king. The prophet's perplexity, however, had its source, according to classical interpretations, in the fact that the people demanded, not a monarch who would abide by biblical principles, but one who would conduct himself on the model of those who governed the nations.[28] If this were to take place, the monarch would believe himself to possess absolute authority, and power would be concentrated in the state in a way that is incompatible with biblical requirements.

It should be recalled, and this has already been stressed above, that Judaism frowns upon the unlimited and massive accumulation of either economic or political power. Even a king shall not amass, without restraint, gold, silver, horses, etc. If he abides by this prescription, he makes available to others the powers that he denies to himself. This too, then, is an application of the principle of the distribution of power.

This principle is also applied, of course, in a more elaborate way, in a political democracy. The separation of powers among the executive, legislative, and judicial branches of government does not merely oppose power with power; it also distributes it. This principle is also expressed in the requirement that heads of state and others who hold political power return to the people, on a regular basis, for election. The concept of election is not biblical, but neither is it incompatible with the biblical perspective which demands, even if in a weaker form, the distribution of power.

The third and, from the Jewish perspective, the best method to limit power is to moralize it. The head of state is required, at all times, to adhere to biblical law. A king is instructed to carry a Torah and to study it with regularity. If Jewish law were integrated into the personality of the sovereign, he would, as a matter of conscience and habit, respond in accordance with the precepts of Judaism. A Jewish character, that is, one which reflects, in action, the values of Judaism, is the best restraint on the misuse or the immoral use of power.

It is useful to note, in this connection, that what distinguishes the messianic personality, according to the Jewish conception, is precisely the fact that, in him, enormous power and unconditional commitment to moral principle are harmoniously blended. This is implied by the passage from Maimonides cited above as well as in the following passage from Isaiah:

> And his delight shall be in the fear of the Lord; and he shall not judge after the sight of his eyes, neither decide after the hearing of his ears; but with righteousness shall he judge the poor and decide with equity for the weak of the earth; and he shall smite the earth with the rod of his mouth, and with the breath of his lips shall he slay the wicked.[29]

It is the Jewish view, then, that the subordination of even enormous power to moral and religious obligations is possible, in the course of human events.

It follows from this discussion that there are two ways to tame power. One is to weaken it, either by building into the social structure opposition between one form of power and another, or by distributing it among different institutions as well as the members of society. The other is to moralize it, that is, to create conditions in which those who wield power will be genuinely moral personalities, so that they will never exercise power over others except in accordance with the requirements of moral law.

An important conclusion follows. Power will not be tamed merely by transferring it. If the point of a revolution is merely to take power from one social class in order to give it to another, and, particularly, if those who inherit the power utilize it to create a totalitarian state, so that political power is once again concentrated in the hands of a few, then the social problems that excessive power generates will not be eliminated—even if that society is organized according to the principle of economic equality. The extent of poverty will be reduced, but exploitation and repression will remain.

VI

Man frequently idealizes that of which he is deprived. Powerlessness may indeed become a value to those who do not possess
power. Poverty has, in this manner and in some quarters, been
turned into an ideal. Judaism has in general resisted this temp-
tation. It does not exalt powerlessness. On the contrary, it ap-
plauds power; it merely requires that its use be guided by precepts
of a moral and religious character.

2

Land

The Jewish people's claim to the Holy Land generates crucial questions. Some are purely philosophical; for instance, what does it mean to have a right? Some have a practical side, such as, what methods may be used to resolve conflicts when different peoples make incompatible claims to ownership of the same object, in this instance, the Holy Land?

No attempt will be made, in response to the practical question, to resolve the conflict by formulating conceptions that, in the case of the sacred territory, will be acceptable to both Jews and their antagonists. We will focus instead on principles, rooted in the Jewish perspective, that prescribe what the Jewish response to such a conflict ought to be. A clear understanding of the Jewish standpoint is indispensable to a rational and, hopefully, a successful approach to the problem.

I

The right which the Jewish people claims, with respect to the Holy Land, is that of ownership. This land, according to biblical testimony, was received from the Divine Being by covenant and is, therefore, the property of the Jewish people. It is true that, in the course of history, other peoples have occupied and administered this territory. From the Jewish vantage point, however, they did so without legitimacy.

25

The notion of property needs to be examined. The statement that a piece of land L is my property means that there exists a standard S which (1) specifies the conditions in which I have a right to L; (2) makes explicit that which I may do with L in virtue of the fact that I have right to it; and (3) declares that everybody else has the obligation not to interfere with my use of L in the authorized way.

1. Any claim to the effect that a person has a certain right presupposes the existence of a source from which the right derives. What is it then that gives sanction to a right and, simultaneously, legitimacy to a claim based on that right? Several theories address this question.

The positive theory defines a right as a privilege conferred by an existing legal system and denies that there are any rights other than legal. There are no transcendental principles, for example, from which rights might spring in contradiction to those generated by the law of the land. An individual has a right to freedom in a democratic society; he does not have it in a totalitarian society. This view is not unpopular among jurists.[1]

The natural law theory claims that there is a source of right other than the positive. Such a theory was presupposed by the authors of the American Declaration of Independence, who wrote, "We hold these truths to be self-evident, that all men are created equal, that they are endowed by their Creator with certain unalienable Rights, that among these are Life, Liberty and the pursuit of Happiness." On this view, the mere act of contemplation reveals immediately (for it is self-evident) that all men have certain rights. Another natural law theory which denies the claim of self-evidence declares that a natural right is one which would be agreed upon by all the members of a society under certain conditions.[2] According to either of these theories, if a legislative body enacts a law which contradicts a natural right, the enacted law is denied legitimacy.

The covenantal theory of rights is theological; it locates the source of right in the will of God. Such a theory must be distinguished from a contractual theory, which is natural rather than covenantal. What people would do if they were to assemble for the purpose of defining the terms of social cooperation follows from facts about the nature of man and society. The sanction of a covenantal right, on the other hand, is rooted not in human nature but in the will of God.

The Jewish claim to the Promised Land is based on all of these sources. There is a positive basis: an international agency, the United Nations, determined that there shall be a Jewish state in the ancient territory of the Jewish people. But this is the weakest basis for the Jewish claim, for it makes the right dependent on what the nations of the world believe, at any moment, to be equitable or, more probably, in their own interests. It is not inconceivable that the nations that conferred legitimacy on the Jewish state, in the first place, will ultimately repudiate it.[3]

More important is the basis for the Jewish claim that is derived from considerations of natural law. Such theories generally declare that all men are entitled equally to life, its opportunities, and, according to some, even its goods. These theories, it is true, were expounded for individuals in the context of a single society. Their principles were regarded as those in accordance with which men form associations in a political community. They can be logically extended, however, to encompass different ethnic or national groups in the international arena. When a people has been denied the right of citizenship over lengthy periods of time in many of the countries in which it was dispersed, and was, in addition, frequently turned into a target of hostility ending finally in a Holocaust, then that people, according to the principle of equality, may claim for itself a land and a state in which it may find security and determine the course of its own destiny. This basis for the claim to the holy land, however, does not necessitate that the Jewish people acquire its ancestral home. Any other land, Argentina or Uganda, for example, would serve the purpose as well. The right to equality would not have been violated if the Jewish people had been assigned territory far removed from the Middle East.

Most important is the Jewish claim that is based on a covenantal right. As a result of the Covenant Between the Parts, the ancient land of Canaan became the promised land. It was subsequently invested, also by covenant, with sanctity; that is to say, the Jew became obligated to abide by the *mitzvot ha-teluyot ba-arez*, the precepts that depend on land. In no other place can the Jew experience that intimacy of involvement with the Divine Being that he can in the land he knows to be sacred. The covenantal right to the land, therefore, is derived from the divine promise and from the obligations, imposed by the Divine Being, to abide by the commandments that are applicable to the land.

Some claim that the Jewish people has a *historic* right to the Holy Land. The emphasis on the historic derives from two considerations: the rejection of the religious perspective, that is, choosing a historical rather than a religious focus, and a commitment to the view that the modern Jewish state must be located on the ancient territory of the Jewish people. What is the meaning of this claim?

It does not mean that the Jewish people was the first and is, therefore, the only legitimate occupant of this domain. According to the biblical account, the land had to be taken, by conquest, from seven other peoples. Nor does this right derive from the circumstance that the Jewish people settled in the land, worked on it, and fought for it over lengthy stretches of time. Were this consideration decisive, it would confer upon other peoples who did exactly the same thing the identical historic right.

There are two ways to interpret the historical claim. First, a historical right is one that a people has possessed throughout the course of history. The difficulty with this interpretation is that, while history may record such a right and witness it, it is not its source. The right would have to be construed as rooted in other considerations, for example, a covenantal commitment. The historical right would accordingly be nothing but the religious right in a historical garb.

The historical right may be understood, alternatively, as rooted in the sequence of events that constitute Jewish history. On one interpretation, these events produced a *subjective* psychological inclination in the Jewish mind to accept, as a homeland, nothing but the ancient ancestral territory. Herzl argued this point. He wrote in *The Jewish State*, "Palestine is an unforgettable historic homeland. The very name would be a marvelously effective rallying cry."[4] But Herzl himself did not regard this circumstance as the source of a right, for in the same work he argued in favor of a Jewish state in Argentina and only reluctantly conceded that the ancestral home had a peculiar attraction which could not be ignored.

According to another interpretation, the sequence of events that constitute Jewish history reveals a unique *objective* relationship between the Jewish people and the land—a relationship that must be acknowledged by the peoples of the world and that could be construed as the source of a right. Martin Buber, for example, speaks of such a relationship.

> Thus from the very beginning the unique association between this people and this land was characterized by what was to be, by the intention that was to be realized. It was a consummation that could not be achieved by the people or the land on its own but only by a fruitful cooperation of the two together. . . . Just as, to achieve fullness of life the people needed the land, so the land needed the people, and the end which both were called upon to realize could only be reached by a living partnership.[5]

But what is the character of this unique relationship, and in what is it rooted?

Buber expressed the view that the unique objective relation that obtains between people and land is a mystery.

> In other respects the people of Israel may be regarded as one of the many peoples on earth and the land of Israel as one land among other lands: but in their mutual relationships and in their common task they are unique and incomparable. And in spite of all the names and historical events that have come down to us, what has come to pass, what is coming and shall come to pass between them, is and remains a mystery. From generation to generation, the Jewish people has never ceased to meditate on this mystery.[6]

Buber further explains that the mystery has a religious basis; God is its source. It is possible, however, to agree with Buber but to substitute, for the suggestion that the relation is a mystery, the view that it is derived from the sanctity of the people and the land. The sanctity of both is expressed in obligation. The people was invested with sanctity at Sinai when it accepted the Decalogue. The land is sacred in the sense that it imposes obligations upon the holy people which are not in force elsewhere. The Holy Land directs a greater challenge to the Jew and inspires a deeper response. Hence, the fulfillment, by the Jew, of his own spiritual potential and, simultaneously, his contribution to the well-being of mankind ultimately depend on his presence on the land.

On this interpretation, the historic right is rooted in the religious right but remains different from it. The religious right derives from the covenant by which this land was assigned to the people of Israel. The historic right arises out of the circumstance that this land and this people have a special relationship in virtue of which the people can find fulfillment and make a maximum contribution to mankind only when it is located on the land. But the special relationship is based on the fact that both people and land are sacred.

2. What is it that belongs to me when I own a tract of land? What is mine is only a set of privileges with respect to that land. In the American legal system, a person who takes title to a parcel of land is frequently barred, by conditions specified in the document of ownership, from doing with it as he pleases. He may not, for example, in certain localities, build either a factory or a two-family dwelling. Further, local, state, and federal authorities have the right to expropriate the land for public use. An individual's ownership of real estate is then never complete; it is invariably shared with others in the community and with government.

Judaism conceives of property in similar terms. When an ancient Jew bought a piece of land, he knew that he could hold it only until the year of jubilee. His ownership allowed him no more than the right to use the land for a period of years. It was on that basis that the price of the parcel was determined.

According to the multitude of years thou shalt increase the

price thereof, and according to the fewness of years thou shalt
diminish the price of it; for according to the number of the
years of the fruits does he sell thee.[7]

The government is also, on the Jewish view, entitled to expropriate
private property. Maimonides, in describing the privilege of the
sovereign, declares, "And he takes fields, olive trees, and vineyards
for his servants when he goes to war."[8] The individual who pur-
chases land, therefore, acquires many privileges with regard to it,
but his ownership is never absolute; others invariably have rights
in it as well.

This conclusion illuminates the meaning of the promise that
the Jewish people would inherit the Holy Land. What was the
intent of the promise? There is a difference between ownership
and possession. A piece of land is owned by an individual who
has a right to it; it may, nevertheless, not be in his possession. He
may have rented it to another; it may have been taken from him
by force. As a result of the Covenant Between the Parts, Abraham
and his descendants became the owners of the Holy Land, and
at the same time, received the promise of ultimate possession.
Now, what kind of ownership was thus acquired by covenant? Or,
to put the question in another way, what kind of possession is
intended in the promise? Two interpretations are possible. (1)
Each parcel of sacred territory will ultimately be occupied by an
individual member of the Jewish people. On this interpretation,
the promise could be fulfilled though the land were governed by
a foreign power. There are several objections to this explication.
First, the possession of every piece of land would be shared by
Jew and non-Jew; for the non-Jewish sovereign has rights in each
parcel as well. Further, the right of expropriation implies that the
sovereign has a stronger claim to the land than does the individual
title-holder. Moreover, Judaism does not require that each tract
in the sacred territory shall be in Jewish hands.[9] It appears necessary therefore to interpret Jewish possession in (2) the public,
rather than the private sense; that is to say, though individual
title-holders may indeed be outside the covenantal community,
the entire land will be possessed by the Jewish people when it is

governed by Jews. In such a case, even when a non-Jew acquires property in the Holy Land, it remains in the possession of the Jew because of the rights in it of the Jewish state.

This discussion has led to a very important conclusion. Part of the meaning of the idea of a Promised Land is that the Jew shall be politically autonomous in the land; that is to say, the right to the Promised Land also means the right to a Jewish state.

3. If an individual possesses a right, others have the obligation not to interfere with his exercise of that right. As one philosopher has explained, a property right is not a relation between an individual and an object, but a relation among an individual, an object, and other individuals,[10] that is to say, others have the obligation not to interfere with the owner in his legitimate use of the object.

A problem arises when one person's claim to a right is denied by others. The Jewish claim to the Promised Land is simply repudiated by the Arabs, and there is no way of refuting their counterclaim to their satisfaction. It is, of course, much more difficult, in a debate concerning rights, to prevail on one of the disputants to admit error than it is in the case of a conflict about matters of fact. In factual debates, the acknowledged method is that of observation and experiment. There are public and objective procedures which, when they are decisive, compel one of the antagonists in the conflict to confess that he is mistaken. There is no comparable method in the case of a conflict over rights. Rights are not subject to observation or manipulation in laboratories. It is nevertheless useful to present the Jewish view on the methods that may be adopted to resolve such a conflict. There are three—the recognition of priorities, compromise, and the use of power. Each will be considered in turn.

II

It is well known that the legitimate rights of individuals frequently contradict each other. Even when neither party to a contested object denies the right of another to it, it is often impossible for both claims to be satisfied. A man finds an object whose owner is identifiable. The finder has the right to proceed with his own affairs, but the loser has the right to have his object returned. Who has a prior right? The Talmud discusses this question extensively.[11] Parents are divorced and both have a right to the children; whose right has more weight? Both the government and an individual have rights to a piece of property. When should one of these rights be assigned precedence? The only time that a question of rights is at all interesting is when it is contested, and that happens often enough to require endless litigation in the courtroom.

The task of adjudication, therefore, involves not merely the decision that, as between a plaintiff and defendant, the right of one must be acknowledged and the other denied, but frequently the determination that while the rights of both must be granted recognition, the claims of one are more commanding. A legal system, in fact, provides both a definition of rights and a standard according to which various rights are assigned priorities. Its latter function enables a society to resolve disputes among its citizens.

The enterprise of resolving a conflict of rights is obviously more difficult when it arises between peoples who base their claims on incompatible standards. Litigants in an American courtroom will submit—or will be compelled to do so—to the decision of a judge who assigns a priority to the claims of one over the other according to prescriptions emerging out of America's legal system. But when Israelis and Arabs demand the identical territory, they do so according to different standards, and neither of them need recognize the legitimacy of the other's claim.

The problem becomes increasingly severe when the two standards are claimed to be absolute because they are based on a transcendental source. If the right to a piece of land is rooted in the will of God, and if two different religious persuasions interpret that will in incompatible ways, there is no way of prevailing upon one group to subordinate its claim to that of the other. The inevitable result may be endless struggle or a decision by both groups that a transcendental problem must receive a transcendental solution. A dramatic example is the existence of a mosque on the sacred mountain in Jerusalem where the ancient Jewish sanctuary, the Holy Temple, was once located. The place is holy to both Jews and Moslems, and each claims a transcendental right to the site. The resolution of this conflict, according to many pious and thinking Jews who wish to avoid ongoing warfare, must await an act of God and the messianic era.

The Jewish people maintains, however, that it has a prior right to the land of Israel—and for two reasons. First, the entire land has the character of sanctity for Jews, while only a few small and limited areas are sacred to members of other faiths. Secondly, even on a nontranscendental basis, the Jewish claim to the land is based on the need for self-preservation; while its possession is hardly relevant even to the well-being, let alone the survival, of the Arabs. If the State of Israel is threatened, the lives of both the state and its citizens are endangered. Furthermore, to the extent that the State of Israel provides a haven for persecuted Jews around the world, the self-preservation of disapora Jewry also requires a Jewish state. For the Jew, therefore, the State of Israel is essential to survival. In the case of the Arabs, on the other hand, given their natural resources and the large domain they occupy and govern, the imposition of Arab control over the land of Israel can supply little more than the satisfaction of an inclination.

III

Another method of resolving disputes is that of compromise. The application of the principle of justice involves the determination that one of two litigants is right and the other wrong. The method of compromise substantially ignores the question of right and wrong; it rather attempts to discover a formula that will yield satisfaction to both litigants. Both of these methods are considered in the Talmud, and there are those who argue that, at least in the case of conflict affecting individuals, it is preferable to compromise.[12]

How shall the principle of compromise be applied to the conflict between Jews and Arabs over the right to the Holy Land? What kind of concessions may Jews make in order to resolve the dispute over the sacred territory? It is clear that Jews cannot assign to another their religious, that is, covenantal, right to this land, because this right is not merely a privilege; it is also an obligation.[13] If a right is only a privilege, it need not be exercised; it may be bartered away. If it is also an obligation, it cannot be exchanged for something else. The Jew does not have the right to dispose of his covenantal obligations.

The Jew could readily compromise on this issue if his right to the land were considered only from a noncovenantal point of view. When he contemplates his rights only insofar as they derive from a positivistic or naturalistic basis, he is able to make concessions because the possibility of doing so is embedded in the system which confers the rights in the first place. A system of positive or natural law usually provides means for the assignment of one's rights to another. One can do so as an expression of generosity, in an exchange, or even to pacify a would-be assailant. Further, a right rooted in either a positivistic or a naturalistic system is merely a privilege which need not be exercised. But there is no way to suspend a covenantal right which is, at the same time, an obligation.

It is possible, within the covenantal framework, however, to make concessions without giving up the right to any portion of the Holy Land or violating the obligation to preserve it within the Jewish domain. Jewish law describes conditions in which the obligation to abide by biblical and rabbinic precepts may be suspended. There is the circumstance known as *pikku'ah nefesh*. Religious laws—those of the Sabbath or *kashrut* for example—may be transgressed if life is threatened, even if death is far from certain. There is the principle of *ya'avor ve-al yehareg*, which applies to a situation in which an individual is threatened with death if he fails to violate a religious precept and which requires the suspension of all but three laws, namely, idolatry, adultery, and murder.

The two principles differ. *Pikku'ah nefesh* is applicable to a situation where death is *possible*, but not *probable*. Every case of internal injury justifies the transgression of the Sabbath, though death is unlikely, because it is an instance of *pikku'ah nefesh*.[14] *Ya'avor ve-al yehareg* applies where death is the *probable* consequence of the refusal to violate a Jewish precept.[15]

Now while one can generally estimate, in the case of an individual, whether the occurrence of death in a certain situation is possible or probable, it is not as easy to determine with accuracy the degree of danger that accompanies a military action, or a political decision which carries with it military implications. Such an estimate is essential because, in a military context, the principle of *pikku'aḥ nefesh* does not apply. A soldier cannot, on religious grounds, refuse to serve in the army or to engage in a battle because doing so represents a threat to life, that is, *pikku'aḥ nefesh*. If such a refusal were legitimate, Judaism could never have sanctioned a war (in which the threat to life is ever present). If, however, the defeat of the army with its attendant destruction and annihilation is probable, the obligation to preserve every portion of sacred territory need not be fulfilled. The principle of *Ya'avor ve-al yehareg* is indeed applicable. It is for this reason that Jews refrained from taking up arms to reclaim the Holy Land throughout the course of diaspora history. Jewish history thus testifies to the Jewish view that the obligation to exercise the right to the Holy Land should be suspended when the end result of such an effort could prove disastrous.

The obligation to possess the Holy Land therefore cannot, by itself, justify a military action or a political decision with military consequences. There is needed, in addition, the determination, on the basis of the best available evidence, that the political or military step to be taken is probably devoid of tragic consequences. It follows that, even from a covenantal, that is, a halakhic, perspective, such a decision must be made by statesmen and military tacticians rather than by rabbis and theologians.

Gush Emunim is a religiously inspired group determined to preserve the West Bank within the boundaries of Israel. Its members point to the sanctity of this territory and the obligation of the Jewish people to retain it within the domain of the Jewish state. A professor at Hebrew University, in a private conversation, declared that this group is in the category of the *rodef*, that is, the man who is pursuing another with the intent to kill who may, according to biblical precept, himself be killed. The professor's identification of Gush Emunim with the *rodef* suggests that the group is threatening the life of Israel and its people and should meet the fate of the *rodef*. Now it is essential to note that the dispute, though expressed in halakhic terms, is not over a halakhic issue. Both the advocates of Gush Emunim and the professor agree that there is a covenantal right to the West Bank and an obligation to exercise it. Both agree that a *rodef* may himself be killed. The argument therefore is not about the law but the fact. Does an unauthorized settlement on the West Bank constitute a threat to the State of Israel, or, conversely, will it strengthen Israel's political and military posture? The abstract principle of Jewish law cannot, by itself, decide the issue. There is needed, in addition, the best political and military knowledge available.

In sum, the Jewish right to the Holy Land and its concomitant obligation are ever present, but compromise is nevertheless possible. Since a political or military step is frequently fraught with danger, the right and its accompanying obligation may often be suspended on the basis of political and military considerations. If they dictate concession, compromise is necessary.

IV

Should a conflict of rights be resolved by the application of power? It is the classic question: does might make right?

Rabbinic Judaism acknowledges that power does have a *role* to play in some circumstances. If an object belongs to no one (i.e., is *hefker*), the one who grasps it first becomes its owner. If two people claim that a piece of real estate is a patrimony, and evidence is not available to establish the truth, Rabbi Naḥman declared *kal de-alim gaver*,[16] it belongs to the stronger. If one occupies a piece of land for three years (also an act of power), the land belongs to him.[17]

But power, on the rabbinic view, is in no case a source of legitimacy. Power never *creates* a right. A distinction must be drawn between a right's sanction and its mode of acquisition. In a political situation, the source of a right may be a system of law which, for example, prescribes that a right is acquired with respect to an ownerless object by an act of power, such as staking out a piece of land. In such a situation, one who performs an act of power gains a right which is generated, not by the act of power, but by the legal system.

The covenant, as developed in Jewish law, the Halakhah, is the *source* of right; the Halakhah, however, prescribes that, in certain contexts, power may be employed to *establish* a right. Consider, for example, the doctrine of Rabbi Naḥman, *kal de-alim gaver*. One interpretation of this principle declares that he who was defeated in a contest of strength may subsequently use force to wrest the object from his opponent.[18] Rabbi Naḥman's principle is then the view that power cannot even establish a right, let alone create one. Another interpretation has it that Rabbi Naḥman's intent is that once a contested property is possessed by force, the loser may not subsequently use force to retrieve it for himself.[19] But this should not be interpreted to mean that power creates but only that it establishes a right. The very same interpreter declares that the successful use of force, in the first instance is, at least to some extent, *evidence* that right is on the side of the victor.

The identical talmudic approach is found in connection with the acquisition of title after occupying a tract of land for an uncontested period of three years. The Mishnah declares that the mere possession of land, if it is unaccompanied by a claim to a right, does not establish a title.[20] The occupant can acquire a title to it only if he claims that he bought it, or that he inherited it, or that he received it as a gift, but that the evidence has been lost. If he makes no such claim, if the sole consideration that he offers is lengthy occupation, title is not his. An act of power does not, then, create a right; it is, at best, evidence for the existence of a right.

What is true in the case of an individual apparently holds for a people as well. There is celebrated midrashic commentary attributed to a Rabbi Isaac.

> The Torah, which is the law book of Israel, should have commenced with the verse "This month shall be unto you the first of the months" [Exodus 12:1], which is the first commandment

given to Israel. What is the reason, then, that it commences with creation? Should the people of the world say to Israel, "You are robbers, because you took by force the lands of the seven nations of Canaan," Israel may reply to them, "All the earth belongs to the Holy One, blessed be He; He created it and gave it to whom He pleased. When He willed, He gave it to them, and when He willed, He took it from them and gave it to us.[21]

The implication of this passage is clear. Force cannot generate a title to a land. Israel's claim to the Holy Land is rooted, not in power, but in the will of God as expressed in a covenantal commitment.

This is not to say that, on the rabbinic view, power lacks the capacity to contribute at all to the character of the relationship between the Jewish people and its land. Maimonides makes it abundantly clear that the conquest of the ancient territory by Joshua and his people conferred upon the land its orginal sanctity.[22] But there is a clear and obvious difference between title to the land and the sanctity of the land. Title to the land derives from the covenantal commitment. The sanctity of the land, which ultimately depends on its actual possession, follows from an act of power. Power is, after all, indispensable to the fact (as opposed to the right) of possession.

A conflict of rights with respect to the Holy Land cannot, therefore, from the Jewish standpoint, be resolved by an act of power.

V

The Jewish people's claim to the Holy Land is strong and persistent. Its strength is derived from a theological source; its persistence is a manifestation of this people's determination to secure the sacred territory as its homeland.

3

Sovereignty

Jewish thought assigns to political sovereignty a theological basis. The idea of a theologically based political arrangement is, of course, unappetizing to the modern mind, which is more comfortable with the notion that government finds its sanction in the will of the people (in the case of democracy) or a historical process (in the case of communism). A theologically sanctioned sovereign is, to the understanding of most people, one who rules, by divine right, as an absolute monarch; but such notions are alien to popular views on legitimate sovereignty.

Notwithstanding, a Jewish conception of sovereignty will be developed here which is explicitly theological; yet it conforms to contemporary political attitudes in that it treats sovereignty as an essentially secular activity. The fact that political arrangements are theologically endorsed encourages opposition to an existing political system, and this provides the most effective obstacle to political absolutism. These conclusions will emerge out of an analysis of the two notions that are central to the concept of sovereignty: authority and power.

I

The term *authority*, in this context, will mean the right to impose obligations. Other senses attach to this word as well. It is sometimes defined in terms of the possession of expertise; for example, an authority on the theory of relativity can answer questions on the subject, and an authority on ethics can resolve complicated moral problems. Authority is sometimes equated with power. A conquering general's authority, insofar as the vanquished are concerned, is construed in terms of the power he wields over them. An employer's authority consists in the economic forces he can bring to bear upon his employees. The term *authority* as it will be used here has neither of these senses. The Jewish political sovereign may not have any special expertise, desirable though it may be; he may not have much power, though power is indeed essential to sovereignty; he nevertheless deserves obedience because he has the *right* to impose obligations.

From whence does this right derive? From the standpoint of Jewish theology, there is but one answer, the divine will. All forms of authority recognized and accepted by Judaism have the identical source. It is the biblical verse "Honor thy father and thy mother"[1] that imposes on the child the obligation to obey his parents. There is nothing intrinsic to the spiritual or biological anatomy of a human being that obligates obedience on the part of progeny. Where, as is often the case contemporaneously, theological and moral bases for filial piety are rejected, respect for parents declines. The right of rabbis to render judgments and issue decrees similarly has a biblical foundation. "According to the sentence of the law that they shall teach thee, and according to the judgment which they shall tell thee, thou shalt do; thou shalt not depart from the sentence which they shall show thee to the right hand, nor to the left."[2] When, for example, the rabbis prescribed the lighting of candles as the Ḥanukkah festival's form of observance, the ritualistic pattern represented an expression of the rabbinic will, but the obligation to obey had its source in the divine will.[3] The authority of a political sovereign also has a biblical basis. "From among thy brethren shalt thou set a king over thee."[4] The ultimate basis for sovereign authority is divine sanction.

Several conclusions follow. First, no human being has an *inherent* right to exercise mastery over another. The fact that one person is the progenitor of another, that he is spiritually more accomplished, that he is superior by some physical, intellectual, or moral standard, or that he occupies a sovereign position in society may *inspire* another to obedience but does not *obligate* it. Authority, that is, the right to impose obligations, does not flow from individual characteristics or the relations that one person has to another. The principle of human equality is not needed to repudiate a claim to political authority. Judaism recognizes that people are, in many ways, unequal. Talent, intellectual capacity, social position are not evenly distributed among the members of society. Notwithstanding, the superman (assuming one exists) does not have an inherent right to dominate another. For Judaism, the right to command derives exclusively from a single source, the will of God.

Second, the divine will mediates the relations of citizen to sovereign. Indeed, the will of God is present in all relations of moral and political obligation, theologically construed. Whenever I perform a duty towards man, I fulfill an obligation to God. This is the meaning of the passage in Baḥya, to which reference has already been made in the first chapter, which declares: "It also follows that no virtue can exist in anyone whose heart is devoid of humility before God."[5] Virtues are associated with the fulfillment of obligations. The just man is one who conforms to the obligation to practice justice, and a generous individual responds to the obligation to assist those in need. But these obligations have God as their source, and the sense of humility is that by which one recognizes them as an expression of God's will. It follows that one cannot possess a religious virtue without a sense of humility.

It may be argued that there is one additional source of obligation, at least in the political arena, namely, the social contract. If a society is viewed as arising out of an agreement which formulates the terms of social association and cooperation, is it not reasonable to assume that such a contractual arrangement itself imposes obligations and confers sovereign authority. While Jewish thinkers have indeed acknowledged the validity of social agreements,[6] they nevertheless regarded sovereign authority as possessing theological roots and the social agreement as effective only to the extent of justifying the selection of one form of government over another and of designating certain individuals rather than others to the role of sovereign. Jewish monarchs were originally

appointed by prophetic designation with confirmation by the Sanhedrin. When these institutions disappeared from Jewish life, they
were replaced by something like the social contract. But, regard-
less of the method employed to organize a government, the basis
for sovereign authority remained the biblical verse, "From among
thy brethren shalt thou set a king over thee."

It follows that no political law or decree has legitimacy if it
contravenes the divine will. A Jewish state may, of course, have
the capacity to compel compliance with its legislation because of
the power concentrated in it, but its laws will not have sanction
unless they are consistent with Jewish religious precepts. Hence,
while the democratic form of government may well be compatible
with Jewish political theory, Judaism cannot regard legislation in
a democracy as acceptable if it merely conforms to the will of the
people. An interesting analogy is afforded by the democratic experience. The nature of laws in a democratic society is often debated. Some believe that the only requirement they must satisfy
is consistency with what the people regard as in their best interests.
Others maintain that they must also conform to a higher moral
code. The Supreme Court, for example, is unique to the American
system of democracy; it is not part of the governmental structure
of other democracies, for example, England and Israel. This court
has the right to declare unconstitutional a law that was approved
by a majority of Congress and which ostensibly reflects the will
of the people. Some political thinkers have objected to the assignment of such extraordinary power to a handful of men and
have argued that the people's will should be the sole controlling
factor. It is evident that, in American democracy at least, the
legislative branch of government is subject to a set of principles
in which greater authority is lodged. The Jewish political conception is analogous. An election process and the social contract out
of which it emerges are essential to the creation of a government,
but that government must remain responsive to those transcendental principles which theology recognizes as the expression of
God's will. Maimonides put it simply.

If one ignores a sovereign edict because he is engaged in the
performance of a *mitzvah* . . . he is free of guilt. When the

master speaks and the servant speaks, the words of the master are to be given priority. Needless to say, if the sovereign's decree is intended to abolish a *mitzvah*, he shall not be obeyed.[7]

It is illuminating to observe in this connection that the principle of the majority by which the will of the people is made explicit in legislation is essentially a means, not an end. It is a method of assuring self-government to the members of society. It is a way of reducing at least the abuses and exploitation from which people suffer in a state where this safeguard is not available. But the application of this principle does not guarantee that the best interests of the people will, at all times, be served. Many a piece of legislation duly approved by a properly constituted legislative body in accordance with the majority principle is neither consistent with the well-being of the community nor with the requirements of morality. Often enough, the laws of a democratic state disenfranchise and provide unequal and hence unjust treatment for large segments of society, for example, laws that deny the ballot to those who are unable to pay a required tax. Laws are also, on occasion, unjust. This is recognized in both Jewish and American political theories; both acknowledge an authority higher than the will of the people.

II

The sovereign, therefore, rules by divine sanction and must be responsive to the divine will. Still, his fundamental aim and his methods are social rather than theological. This is basically the difference between political and rabbinic authority. Rabbis are concerned primarily with the application of biblical and rabbinic precepts to human events. They seek to embody the will of God in human conduct, interpersonal relations, and community patterns. They seek to make God's presence felt in human affairs. The sovereign, on the other hand, though he has a divine mandate, is instructed to introduce laws designed to accomplish essentially social ends. It is not so much God's will as the needs of society to which he must respond through legislation. As one classic rabbinic thinker put it

But the purpose of the judge [rabbinic] and the Sanhedrin was to judge the people according to truth and justice in order that the divine element may cling to us [the Jewish people]. . . . But kings were appointed to arrange the political order and to do what was needed because of the times.[8]

It follows that the political structure of the Jewish state is not fixed for all times. Theological principles are eternal and categorical; political structures are transitory and tentative—they change from generation to generation, and must always be adjusted according to the exigencies of the time. Political imperatives are legislated in the light of specific goals which, in turn, reflect what people regard as their fundamental social needs. A monarchy will be chosen, as Hobbes argued, if the primary concern is security; a democracy will be selected if priority is assigned to freedom. Men will opt for a socialistic society if they seek a more uniform distribution of economic goods; they will choose capitalism if they place greater emphasis on freedom in the marketplace. A variety of circumstances prompt a people to adopt a specific social objective, and the laws of a society generally reflect the choice that was made.

The biblical sanction of sovereignty is then the principle that conveys to the Jewish community, when it recognizes certain objectives as desirable, the right to choose political arrangements suitable for their realization. Monarchy is not the only type of government acceptable to Jewish theological thought. The point has already been stated above; it must be emphasized. It is true that the biblical endorsement of political sovereignty occurs in the statement "From among thy brethren shalt thou set a king over thee," in which the word *king* is explicitly used. This imperative, however, should be understood as primarily providing the authority to create a political sovereign and not necessarily as the requirement that the sovereign shall take the form of a monarch (though in the messianic era the concept of the messianic king appears to be essential). A talmudic passage, for example, in a discussion of the difference between a judgment rendered by a *bet din* (a Jewish court of law) and one pronounced by a sovereign, places Joshua, the successor to Moses and a judge, in the category of a monarch.[9] It follows that the Talmud does not assign to the word *king* in the biblical precept a literal meaning. Maimonides declared that the Jewish leaders of the ancient Babylonian community, none of whom was ever so designated, enjoyed the status of kings in that they had the right to judge and to execute their judgments in the manner of kings.[10] Maimonides also asserts that one of non-Jewish identity may not be designated to any position of authority in Jewish life—such as king, president, judge, or captain—and explains that this prohibition is to be inferred from the previously cited biblical precept.[11] Maimonides, then, also understands the word *king* in a generic way. A talmudic commentator, Meiri, declared that the laws of sovereignty hold at all times and grants to Jewish leaders of every generation the right to punish and to impose the death penalty in the fashion of a king.[12] Again, the biblical precept is assigned a broad connotation. It is understood as commanding sovereignty and not necessarily monarchy. The sovereign may be a king or even a combination of a president, prime minister, and Knesset.

III

Implicit in the doctrine that the sovereign's primary objective is social rather than theological is the view that the Jew lives in two domains—the natural and the transcendental, the city of man, which is organized according to purposes that emerge out of the human condition and the nature of society, and the city of God, arranged according to Torah precepts whose function it is to bring the individual Jew and the Jewish community into close and intimate relation with the Divine Being. Activity in the natural world must, of course, be limited and bounded by transcendental principles. One could not, for example, permit work on the Sabbath when no threat to life exists on the grounds that it will serve the national purpose. But there are occasions when the Halakhah is not directly applicable or when it suspends itself in order to permit the application of a natural principle. Transcendental precepts, for example, do not prescribe a schedule for a war tax or determine that drivers should keep to the right or left lane of a highway.

The suspension of halakhic principles occurs in instances where a threat to life exists and where, for example, the laws of medicine and biology become authoritative. Such a suspension could take place for individuals as well as communities. There are also cases where the Halakhah itself permits the sovereign to set aside a halakhic precept in order the better to achieve a halakhic objective. This happens when the principle of *tikkun ha-olam*, the moral improvement of society, is relevant. Maimonides, for example, writes, "He who kills without leaving clear evidence or without having been warned or even in the presence of one witness . . . may be killed by the sovereign authority for the improvement of society and as the times may require."[13] There is a Jewish legal principle which prohibits imposing the death penalty on a murderer unless he attacked his victim in the presence of two witnesses and was warned, antecedent to the crime, not to do so. The strict and unexceptional application of this principle would permit the proliferation of murderers and leave the Jewish community defenseless. The sovereign was accordingly permitted to impose the death penalty to preserve the moral character of society.

Further, the transcendental is the arena to which the Jew responds selflessly; the natural is the domain in which he is permitted to pursue goals inspired by considerations of self-interest. In the city of God, the human posture must be that of responsibility and unselfishness; in the city of man, one may pursue the fulfillment of his own needs and assign priority to that which gives him satisfaction. There is a realm of freedom in Jewish life—in that sense of freedom according to which every person may do as he wishes. Such freedom is available to the individual. Rashi, on the verse "And thou shalt proclaim liberty [*deror*] throughout the land to all the inhabitants thereof,"[14] points out that the Hebrew word for "liberty" (*deror*) that occurs here has precisely that connotation. There is an area in which the Jew is authorized to act according to considerations of self-interest. Such a right is also available to the Jewish people considered as a single entity. Not all of a people's communal life is bound by obligatory precepts. The right of the people to do that which it regards as in its best interests, that is, the people's freedom, is presupposed in the biblical precept authorizing sovereignty. The ideal sovereign acts invariably, when permitted to do so by transcendental principles, according to the national interest.

There is still another difference between the natural and the transcendental spheres that deserves attention. A representative of the transcendental, a rabbi for example, cannot retain authority if he explicitly denies or rejects the principles of the domain he claims to represent. He could not, at least in a traditional context, be both a rabbi and an atheist. It is otherwise with a political sovereign. It is certainly possible, from a logical perspective at least, for him to regard his authority as theologically sanctioned even while he is openly hostile to Judaism. One may argue that such a person should not be designated to leadership in Jewish life, as Maimonides declares explicitly,[15] but it is clear that the prophetic books of the Bible acknowledge the sovereignty of many such individuals.

Notwithstanding these differences, however, the two domains remain connected. Cooperation in the enterprise of realizing the religious objective is, at least, desirable on the part of the political sovereign. He must strive to create conditions in which the principles of Jewish life could be embodied in social patterns. It was the sovereign who was granted the authority to punish an offender who threatened the moral and religious life of the community in the event that the Halakhah prevented such punishment from being carried out. It was the sovereign (King Solomon, for example) who had the power and the resources to build the Holy Temple which was so crucial to the development of the religious life of the community. The Jew must act upon transcendental principles in the natural world, and it is the sovereign who has the capacity and the obligation to mold the natural world in a manner that would make it available to the practice of these principles.

The implications of this discussion for the modern State of Israel are clear. The government has the obligation to legislate and to act in a manner that is consistent with the national interest. It must do so in accordance with the best information made available by economic, sociological, political, and military science. The preservation of the state and the well-being of its people are its paramount considerations. It must also constantly strive to create conditions in which the practice of Judaism would be supported and encouraged.

IV

Sovereignty also means power. The organization of natural conditions to achieve national objectives requires massive quantities of various forms of power—military, economic, political, cultural. The principal problem is that of making sovereign power coextensive with sovereign authority. Power has the tendency to break through boundaries of legitimacy—and this is especially the case with state power, which, if not effectively restrained, tends towards absolutism.

First, what are the limits of sovereign power, that is, what are the boundaries beyond which a sovereign may not use power to enforce authority? Jewish thought does not supply a precise answer to this question. Several observations, however, are in order. First there is a talmudic debate as to the extent to which even a prophetically designated monarch may go in the exercise of power. It is based on the passage in I Samuel in which, in response to the people's demand that he appoint a king to govern them, the prophet enumerated a list of monarchial prerogatives. The sage Samuel declared that the king was permitted all that the prophet described. Rav's opposing view holds that it was not the prophet's intention to sanction such conduct, but only to stress the fact that the monarch was to be treated with reverence.[16] The debate on the limits of sovereign power is ancient in rabbinic literature.

There is a second consideration. It has been noted above that when the institutions of the prophet and the Sanhedrin disappeared from Jewish life, the leaders of the Jewish community, who according to the Halakhah enjoyed sovereign status, were appointed by the people. Rabbi Abraham Isaac Kook declared that in the absence of a prophetically designated king, it is the people who assumed sovereign authority. In connection with the legislative authority of the sovereign, for example, he writes, "I believe that, when there is no king, because the legislation of the commonwealth relates also to the general well-being of the people, all legislative rights return to the people."[17] Further, the suggestion is plausible that the sovereign chosen by the people is their agent, and accordingly, that his rights may be limited to those which the people are willing to grant. This is one possible interpretation of the relation between people and sovereign.[18] If this is indeed the case, no one designated by the people may exercise more power than that which it willingly grants.

We return to the original problem—how is power to be restrained? There are two forces that resist the undue expansion of sovereign power. One has already been noted; it is religious in character. The religious community, in its totality, is heir to the prophetic mission, often political in nature, of providing opposition to sovereign power. The pious individual will not abide by the sovereign will when it contradicts the divine will. Those who are moved by religious commitment will reject a law of the state if the result of its observance is the violation of a Torah precept. A Jewish sovereign power, even if it is secular in orientation, will recognize and respond to the force that is concentrated in the religious community and will invariably try to avoid legislation that will arouse opposition and hostility. This is certainly the case in the contemporary Jewish state. To the extent that any government must be responsive to its citizenry, and insofar as a democratic government is particularly so, Israel's religious community will always be a factor in political considerations—with or without the existence of a religous political party. The second is political. If the citizens of a Jewish state arrive at the realization that the sovereign power has overstepped the boundaries of legal propriety, they may rise in opposition.

The religious basis for disobedience is, of course, more effective than the political. The motivation to oppose unacceptable legislation is much stronger among those who have a religious commitment than it is for those who seek to maintain a cherished political order. In addition, opposition on religious grounds normally does not require the deliberation that is essential to politically prompted disobedience. The religiously minded individual will simply reject the demand by a sovereign power that a Torah precept be violated when no threat to life exists. Religious principles are, in most instances, readily applied. When, however, sovereign action appears to be inconsistent with political requirements, the would-be opponent must first determine that such action is indeed illegitimate and, in addition, that it is desirable, by some pragmatic standard, for him to disobey. While the religious domain is one of conscience, where frequently little room is left for deliberation, the political realm is one of rights, in which calculation is inevitable. Citizens may decide that, notwithstanding sovereign transgression, it is advantageous not to insist on accepted political procedures.

V

The Jewish idea of political sovereignty is ancient and yet modern. It is certainly consistent with the practice of democracy and even strengthens the democratic principle of government by providing a stronger basis for political opposition than that which is available to its secular counterpart.

4

Equality

It is well known that Judaism does not insist on the universal and exceptionless application of the principle of equality. Sometimes priority is assigned to the Jew over the non-Jew and, on occasion, to the Jewish male over the Jewish female. A Jew, for example, may not steal from anyone, including the non-Jew who violates the minimal Noachide commandments;[1] but he must be more concerned with safeguarding the property of fellow Jews.[2] Both men and women, according to Jewish law, have the right to possess property, while only men have the right to inherit it, if the deceased has male heirs.[3] There remain nevertheless, after recognizing the ways in which Judaism judges human beings to be unequal, some ways in which they are regarded as equal.

The concept of human equality has both a descriptive and a prescriptive sense. Descriptively, it means that people are, as a matter of fact, equal. Prescriptively, it means that human beings should be treated as equals. Both of these are affirmed in Jewish thought.

I

We may begin with descriptive equality. It is popularly held that men are equal in the sense that all are created *be-zelem Elohim*, in the image of God. All men are held to possess a certain unique

52

spiritual quality. According to the classic view, this quality is man's intellectual capacity. Rashi, for example, interprets the verse "We will make man in our image, after our likeness" to mean "with the power to comprehend and to discern."[4] But it is important to remember that intellectual ability is not equally distributed among men. Intelligence tests exhibit the varying degrees in which it is found. What then happens to the assertion that men are equal by this standard?

This objection is relevant not merely with respect to the human property of intelligence but to any view that claims equality for some essential human characteristic. The doctrine of equality as affirmed in the theory of democracy is vulnerable to similar criticism. Human qualities are possessed in varying degrees. Not only intelligence but health, physical strength, even such pedestrian qualities as weight and height are unequally distributed. A passage in the Mishnah makes this point in theological terms, "If a man strikes many coins from one mold, they all resemble one another, but the Supreme King of Kings, the Holy One, blessed be He, fashioned every man in the stamp of the first man, and yet not one of them resembles his fellow,"[5] and this judgment is intended to apply to more than man's physical features.

A popular defense of human equality is made on the grounds that, while individual traits are indeed exemplified in unequal degrees, men are equal on balance. One person has more intelligence; another greater physical powers; a third more artistic talent. If a sum were taken of the numerical values which measure the qualities possessed by each individual, they would be found to be substantially the same. An English thinker pressed for this view.

Nature hath made man so equal, in the faculties of the body and mind; as that though there be found one man sometimes manifestly stronger in body, or of quicker mind than another; yet when all is reckoned together, the difference between man and man is not so considerable.[6]

This suggestion, however, is not merely false; it is utterly meaningless. There is no method available for adding the numerical values assigned to each human quality in such a way that this claim could even be tested. One can attach a number to intellectual ability through intelligence testing and another to physical strength by some acceptable gymnastic standard. But taking the sum of these two numbers is a senseless procedure; it means nothing at all.

Advocates of human equality have adopted a different approach. They distinguish the possession of a property from the degree of its exemplification. An object can be red but an idea cannot; an animal has the power of sensation but a stone does not; the human being possesses intelligence but a vegetable does not. Now, while it is true that there are different degrees of redness, sensibility, and intelligence, the property of *possessing* any one of these qualities is manifested equally in all instances in which they are exemplified. One philosopher, arguing along similar lines, identifies as a range property one that is not subject to quantitative distinctions and declares that a range property is possessed equally by all its members.

> The property of being in the interior of the unit circle is a range property of points in a plane. All points inside this circle have this property although their coordinates vary within a certain range. And they equally have this property, since no point interior to a circle is more or less interior to it than any other interior point.[7]

A similar analysis may be given for the property of *zelem Elohim*, the divine image. This property, whatever it may be, can be formulated as a range property exemplified equally in all human beings.

Maimonides describes still another characteristic in regard to which the judgment of equality can be made. In a passage dealing with freedom of the will, he writes, "Every man is capable of being righteous like Moses our teacher or a scoundrel like Jeroboam."[8] Here men are judged equal in the possession of *moral potential*. Men do not equally possess intellectual or physical potential; they are not endowed equally with the capacity to become a Maimonides or a Samson. Moreover, men do not possess equally the capacity for *moral achievement*. The moral quality of an individual can, after all, be viewed as dependent on either of two factors, the intention that precedes his actions and the results of his actions—or indeed on both. It is possible to intend to perform an act advantageous to others but to achieve injurious results instead. An act of charity may lead the recipient to squander his acquisition on liquor or drugs with eventual harm to himself and his family. It is also possible for an act to have happy results without these having been intended by the agent. One may give philanthropically, not for the sake of helping those afflicted, but in response to social pressures. Now it is clear that human beings are not equal by the standard of moral results. It is simply not possible for everyone to be the author of actions equivalent, in their human consequences, to those performed by Moses, namely, leading an enslaved people to freedom and giving them a Torah. Equality with Moses can be achieved, however, if the emphasis is placed on intention. Each human being is equally endowed with the potential to perform actions motivated by commitment to moral principle. By this standard too, all men—Jews and non-Jews, men and women—are equal.

In sum, there are two ways in which the descriptive judgment of equality may be made. First, human beings possess equally some trait which derives from their possession of the image of God, though they differ in the degree to which they possess it. Second, all men have equal potential for commitment to moral precept, though they differ in the extent of moral achievement.

II

There are important standards, however, with respect to which Judaism judges men to be unequal. One of these has already been noted. The potential for moral intention is equal in all men; its manifestation in achievement is exhibited unequally. But even when equality cannot be attributed to all mankind, it can, on occasion be assigned to large classes of people. Thus, Rabbinic

Judaism declared that each one who acts in conformity to religious precepts out of commitment to the will of God has equal spiritual worth.

> A favorite saying of the rabbis of Yavneh was: I am God's creature and my fellow is God's creature. My work is in town and his work is in the country. I rise early for my work and he rises early for his work. Just as he does not presume to do my work, so I do not presume to do his work. Will you say that I do much and he does little? We have learned: one may do much or one may do little, it is all one provided he directs his heart to heaven.[9]

The class of pious and moral individuals is clearly smaller then the human race, but by the standard of spiritual worth, all in this class are equal.

There is yet another criterion that confers equality on a limited group. Every human being possesses a degree of sanctity that depends on the number of biblically prescribed obligations he is assigned. Thus, the greater sanctity of the Jew in comparison with the non-Jew derives from the fact that the former has a burden of six hundred and thirteen commandments as against seven for the latter. Of course, there is another form of sanctity that attaches to the Jew with respect to which Jews are unequal, namely, the sanctity that flows from religious conduct. Not all in the Jewish community are equally pious. Nevertheless, the sanctity that is dependent on the extent of religious obligation is a quality equally distributed among all in the class of those who carry the same number of religious duties.

III

The principles of prescriptive equality do not derive from the *facts* of descriptive equality, though they depend on them. The obligation to treat others equally does not have its source in the circumstance that men are, *in fact*, equal by certain standards. To the religiously minded individual, there is but one source for all obligation, namely, the will of God. Even if men were unequal in every important way, it is conceivable that the divine will might still impose on mankind the duty to treat others equally. Nevertheless, the elements of descriptive equality are important for the imperatives of prescriptive equality; for they often serve to define the class of beings to whom the obligations of prescriptive equality are relevant. For example, the possession of intelligence and moral potential characterizes a class of creatures (all men) who must be treated equally in certain ways. One may not, for example, steal from anyone who has those traits. Hence, Maimonides declares that the principle "Thou shalt not steal" is to be applied even to those who violate the basic Noachide commandments.[10] Every human being has an equal right to his property, and its appropriation without his consent constitutes theft. Membership in the covenant with the concomitant obligation to fulfill the full set of biblical commandments defines still another class whose members are entitled to equal treatment by all in their community. Thus, while the payment of interest on a loan is a perfectly acceptable and legitimate business procedure, a Jew may not require such a payment from a fellow Jew—and all Jews are equal in this regard.

IV

The imperatives of prescriptive equality must be derived from ethical and religious principles of which they are integral parts; for the principle of equality is as such, not affirmed explicitly in classic Jewish thought, in either the descriptive or the prescriptive form, as it is in the case of the theory of democracy.

The most obvious moral principle to which equality belongs as an essential part is justice. Any law which singles out an individual or a group for preferential or harsh treatment is unjust because it does not apply equally to all. Maimonides puts it as follows:

But if a king takes a courtyard or field of one of the citizens, contrary to the law he has promulgated, he is deemed a robber, and the original owner may recover it from anyone who buys it from the king. The general rule is this: Any law promulgated by the king to apply to all and not to one person alone is not deemed robbery. But whatever he takes from one particular person only, not in accordance with a law known to everyone but by doing violence to the person, is deemed robbery.[11]

There are two other moral principles to which equality belongs as a component part. Before identifying them, a prefatory remark is in order. In one respect, the Jewish principle of equality differs from its American counterpart. In a democracy, this demand is made primarily of society's institutions; for example, men shall be treated with equality before the law or assigned equal weight in an election process. Democracies may, of course, urge and encourage their citizens to apply the egalitarian principle in their relations to each other, but they do not demand it. Judaism makes this a requirement in individual conduct as well.

It does this in the case of the principle of humility, which, on one of its interpretations,[12] requires that a person shall not view himself as superior to another because of more abundant possessions or greater achievements. It is true that the principle of humility is not precisely an expression of the principle of equality. The latter requires that all men are to be regarded as equal to each other; the former that all men are to be perceived as *at least one's* equal, that is to say, one may regard others as unequal to him so long as he assigns higher value to them, and, further, he need not see his fellow men as equal to each other so long as he perceives them as equal to himself. Nevertheless, the principle of equality is an essential component of the principle of humility. Anyone who regards others as neither inferior nor superior, that is, as equal, to himself is an humble man.

This egalitarian attitude, like the one which inheres in the principle of justice, is applicable not only to the members of the Jewish community, but to all mankind. The biblical passage which declares that Moses was the most humble of men,[13] or the rabbinic precept which requires that a person shall be very very meek,[14] does not distinguish between humility in relation to members of the Jewish community and those beyond it. On the contrary, the

Maimonidean comment on the rabbinic admonition cited here indicates that the imperative of humility must be applied to those outside the boundaries of Jewish life as well. In other words, the principle of equality contained in the concept of humility is universal.[15]

Still another moral principle contains the precept of equality but, in rabbinic tradition, it is limited to the Jewish community. This is the principle of love for the neighbor. Nahmanides explains the biblical verse which prescribes love to mean that a Jew's concern for his neighbor's welfare should equal his concern for his own.[16] Maimonides interprets this verse in the same way. He writes, "He must therefore speak in his [the neighbor's] praise and be as concerned about his money as he is about his own money and honor."[17] In these respects, therefore, he must regard others in his community as equal to himself. Another rabbinic interpretation explains this celebrated biblical verse to mean that he must treat a neighbor as he expects the neighbor to treat him.[18] Maimonides, in another location, adopts this interpretation as well, "All the things that you want others to do for you, do them for others."[19] Thus the claim of others in my community on me is equal to my claim on them.

V

It is important to stress an idea alluded to above, namely, that the obligations of prescriptive equality need not depend on the facts of descriptive equality, that Judaism could demand equal treatment even if men were not equal by any important and relevant standard. With respect to the precept of equality that emerges out of the principle of humility, Nahmanides tells us,

> Every man should be great in your eyes. If he is wise or wealthy, it is your duty to honor him. If he is poor and you are richer or wiser than he, consider that you are more guilty and he more innocent than you.[20]

The point here is that, for Nahmanides, the humble person does not engage in an appraisal to determine that others are, in fact, his equal (or his superior) by some objective and relevant standard. To the contrary, for the humble, the facts are unimportant. Genuine humility involves the deliberate adoption of an attitude. The imperative of equality that flows from it is rooted in a theoretical construction, a legal fiction, a declaration, independent of facts, that each person is to be regarded *as if* he were his equal. I must perceive and treat men as my equals whether they are equal to me or not.

It is important to stress that, in Judaism, it is not the *fact* but the *judgment* of equality that is the social objective. I can subjectively make this judgment, though I recognize that it is not true. In fact, Judaism requires both, that is, the affirmation that men differ by certain standards and that I must treat them as my equals nevertheless.

This dual approach leaves room for criteria of excellence which are so important in Jewish life. The saintly personality who devotes his life to Torah—its study and the application of its precepts in conduct—has greater worth than the profligate who immerses himself in the pursuit of pleasure. The just man is infinitely more valuable than the thief. Sanctity, piety, and moral conduct are exemplified, in varying degrees, in different men. The Jewish emphasis on inequality which encourages the struggle for self-improvement is then, from the moral standpoint, as important as is the stress on equality.

Indeed, its simultaneous insistence on equality and inequality is precisely that which distinguishes the Jewish concept of equality from its American counterpart. Judaism affirms standards; it seeks excellence. It looks for the constant, uninterrupted spiritual growth of those who identify with it. It achieves this by recognizing differences and by the judgment that some are better than others, thereby motivating all to strive for the ideal. This approach differs radically from that adopted by advocates of equality in its American form who pursue what has been called the leveling of American society. They push for the application of the principle of equality beyond the boundary even of its reasonable application. In America, this idea has come to mean that mankind must create the social conditions in which all men will achieve equality in fact, though this enterprise may well throttle the attainment of excellence. It also means that different patterns of living shall be judged equal in value. The diverse religions are generally regarded as so many roads to the same objective, and different moralities are often judged to be equally valid. This conclusion is repugnant to Jewish life. There are differences and they must be recognized even while we are instructed to perceive others and to respond to them as our equals.

VI

In some ways, men are equal. Even if they are not, we are, in many ways, obligated to *regard* them as *our* equal. It is not the *fact* that is crucial, but the *obligation*. The perception of equality, like the recognition of inequality, is essential to moral and religious living.

5

Justice and Equality

Universality is an essential component in the concept of justice. A law cannot be regarded as just unless, in some sense, it applies to all members of a society for which it is enacted. This indeed is the view of Maimonides. In a passage in his compendium to which reference has already been made, where he discusses patterns of taxation, he writes,

> The general rule is this: Any law promulgated by the king to apply to all and not to one person alone is not deemed robbery. But whatever he takes from one particular person only, not in accordance with a law known to everyone but by doing violence to the person, is deemed robbery.[1]

It is then the universal applicability of law that is at least an essential condition of its being just. If, contrariwise, an edict were promulgated for a single individual or group—whether advantageously or disadvantageously—it is not just.

It is necessary to explicate this principle of universality which, while it elicits popular approval, conceals a nest of difficulties.

I

In the first place, the requisite universality cannot be merely logical. In truth, all laws, whether they are of the scientific, moral,

62

or political variety, whether they are just or unjust, are universal in form. Any statement has the character of logical universality if it conforms to the following pattern: "All who have property A have property B." Every law, no matter how unjust, can be written in this form. Examples abound, and just a few will suffice. "All Jews have to pay a special head tax"; "All Jews may not be property owners"; "All blacks may not sit in the front section of public vehicles."

The universality which Maimonides requires, therefore, cannot then be merely logical or formal. It does not refer to a structural character of the formula in which the law is expressed. The required universality appears to be substantive as well. It seems that what Maimonides requires is distributive equality; that is, a just law is one that, at the very least, is *equally* applicable to every member of society. If any person or group of persons is excluded from its benefits or exempt from its obligations, it is inherently unjust. This interpretation, however, is not much of an improvement. In the first place, it is common knowledge that many laws which are generally accepted as just are not applicable to all. Benefits, for example, are often unequally distributed. Social legislation provides for the poor and deprived, but is unavailable for those who are comfortable and is certainly denied to the opulent. This is true of obligations as well. Income taxes are graduated and imposed in a manner proportional to the earnings of the citizen, while some, by virtue of incapacity, are relieved of the burden entirely. If a military conscription were instituted limiting induction into the armed forces to those between the ages of eighteen and twenty-five, it would not be perceived as unjust, though others, somewhat older, might be even more qualified to do battle. But, further, as noted above, Judaism itself distributes, according to halakhic precept, benefits and burdens unequally. In ancient Jewish society, only the Levites, whose status was acquired by birth, were entitled to receive an annual tithe. Everyone was obligated to return to a fellow Jew an object that he lost except a priest, if the object was located on a cemetery (to avoid spiritual pollution), or a sage (if returning it was not appropriate to one of his status).[2] A scoundrel (*rasha*) was not entitled to a whole spectrum of privileges that were the prerogatives of other members of society.[3]

The problem of delineating the element of equality as it enters as a component into the concept of justice is not novel in social philosophy. Since ancient days, philosophers have struggled with it. There has been general recognition that inequalities exist even in a just society. For example, one of the two main principles of justice, as expounded by John Rawls, is that existing social inequalities must be of advantage to all and accessible to all.[4] But whatever qualifications must be introduced to ensure that injustice will not be the result, the inevitable occurrence of inequalities, even in distribution, is acknowledged and is seen to be compatible with a just society. Judaism does not dispute this conclusion.

The proposed solution to this dilemma is ancient in origin. The formulation of equality as a principle of justice should read: equality for those who are equal.[5] Unfortunately, this statement of the principle is equally problematic. The principle enjoins prescriptive equality, that is, equality of treatment, to those who are descriptively equal, that is, to those who are, as a matter of fact, equal, by some criterion. But a multitude of criteria are available. If each one is acceptable, then all societies, no matter what their social organization, so long as their laws are logically consistent, would have to be recognized as just, because such laws generally embody some standard. One would then have to sanction as just, laws which require preferential treatment for any group in society—and in a manner which normally would not be construed as just. Notwithstanding, this formula, namely, "equality for those who are equal," is inevitable.

This follows, in the first place, from purely logical considerations. The group whose members are entitled to equal treatment must be identified. Clearly, nonhuman animals are not to be included in the favored group. Neither would membership be granted to those who, for whatever reason, are not capable of exercising rights or fulfilling obligations. Infants, for example, need not serve in the military, nor are they entitled to vote. Criminals are also excluded from many of the privileges extended to other members of society. It is clear that while prescriptive equality is not deducible from descriptive equality, it is logically related to it, that is to say, it is necessary to identify some trait which belongs to all the members of a class whom we are directed to treat with equality. Hence, from a purely logical point of view, to the extent that the class of those who are deserving of equal treatment must be characterized, the formula of distributive justice must be: equality to those who are equal.

But there is a second factor which recommends the acceptance of the formula of justice under present discussion, namely, *merit*. It is generally recognized that some are more deserving than others of advantages available in society, and that any definition of justice must take the element of merit into account. The delineation of merit, as it is related to distributive justice, has been debated extensively in recent years. Some have argued that the standard that defines merit in an academic context, for example, is purely intellectual. Students with the highest scores on entrance examinations are more deserving of admission to universities; teachers with the best grades on competitive examinations have a greater claim to teach in the classroom. Others, who are disadvantaged when a merit system with an intellectual bias is employed, have argued that merit is also somehow related to degree of repression. Those who, in the past, have suffered the most because of social failures are, by way of compensation, entitled to the most. Advocates of this concept of merit have, accordingly, proposed that members of minority groups are deserving of opportunities for advancement even if, in intellectual contests, their performance is not distinguished. But whatever the concept of merit one may be inclined to introduce as a basis for judging what a person deserves, it is clear that some such standard is indispensable and that the formula "equality to those who are equal," according to some criterion of merit, is inevitable.

A variety of principles of merit are operative in every society, and these reflect diverse forms of inequality that are exemplified in social patterns. According to one conception of merit, a parent is justified in leaving an inheritance to his children rather than to strangers, or if, for some reason, he designated someone beyond the boundaries of his family as a recipient of his beneficence, the sum allocated to the stranger will normally be small in comparison with that received by his progeny. According to another conception of merit, a salary is given to one who is employed only if he fulfills the terms and conditions of employment. In conformity with a third conception, a medical position on a hospital staff will be assigned to one who is most capable of contributing to the health of patients. By still another, those with the greatest number of family responsibilities are exempt from military service. Each one of these instances reflects a different criterion of merit. In one, merit is defined in terms of biological relation or perhaps intensity of love; in another, it is services rendered; in the third, the focus is competence; in the next, it is considerations of compassion. There are many more, and they need not be enumerated. It is clear that merit is an essential component in the concept of justice.

Judaism too incorporates a variety of merit criteria into its system of justice. I will focus on two which serve as a basis for the formulation of the laws of Judaism. It is a biblical imperative, for example, that a Jew shall not accept interest on a loan from a fellow Jew.[6] There is nothing inherently unjust and immoral in the act of demanding such a reward. Indeed, it is accepted practice among many civilized and moral societies to do so; within the Jewish community it remains nevertheless unjust. Evidently, the Halakhah holds that certain characteristics uniformly present among members of the Jewish community, but absent in others, entitle them to special treatment from their coreligionists. Just as a parent cannot be charged with injustice if he chooses to provide for his children with greater magnanimity than he is prepared to display elsewhere, so is the conduct of a Jew consistent with justice if he relates to a Jew with greater generosity than to others.

What is the element that is characteristic of those who belong to the Jewish community in virtue of which they may expect preferential treatment within that community? It may be any one of several and perhaps all of them. The Jew possesses a certain degree of sanctity which belongs to him, and in an amount equal to every other Jew, in virtue of his membership in that community. Each Jew must experience a special feeling for his confreres which is expressed talmudically in the imperative requiring *shittuf bi-za'ar*, partnership in pain.[7] The Jew is obliged to sense a special obligation towards his fellow Jew in accordance with the rabbinic dictum, "All Jews are responsible one for another."[8] But whatever the special character may be, the relation of Jew to Jew parallels in some sense the relation that obtains among members of an intimate family group. It is a relation that imposes obligations upon Jews toward those within their community from which those beyond its borders are excluded.

We shall identify the community in which concrete manifestations of love are obligations as a *love community*. The general view is that a gesture of love is one that is performed voluntarily, even spontaneously. It is generally held that a person can be encouraged, inspired, urged to exhibit love, but that he cannot be commanded to do so. Judaism maintains that the members of the Jewish community are obligatory objects of love and spells out in detail the manner in which that love is to be displayed.

We may put this in another way. Love is essentially a feeling, an emotion, which cannot be generated by legislation. While there are a variety of religions that advocate its exemplification in human affairs, they do not expect political communities to impose expressions of love as legal imperatives. Enforcing relations of love beyond those voluntarily assumed, for instance, in the marital state, is normally held to be excluded from the prerogatives of a sovereign entity. Social policies over which governments preside are generally limited to moral issues which are associated with man's humanity rather than with forms of conduct that arise out of sentimentality. Judaism has adopted another approach. It recognizes that love may be expressed on two levels—as a fact and as a norm, as an emotion and in obligatory conduct. It describes the Jewish people as a love community and demands, as a matter of obligation, that acts of love be performed among its members. The failure to do so is condemned as an injustice.

If one would argue that indeed expressions of love are obligatory, from the Jewish standpoint, towards mankind in general, the obvious response is that love can be exhibited in degrees and in a variety of forms, and that the love obligation that Judaism imposes within the Jewish community is the correlative of an emotion that is deeper and more demanding than that which must be evinced in other relationships.[9] Indeed, the love which a Jew is duty-bound to exhibit to a fellow Jew and the concomitant obligations parallel, though are not identical to, the feelings and obligations that are normally characteristic of an intimate family group. The point is that, in the Jewish perspective, justice prescribes obligations universally and equally, among the members of a love community—taking into account that different degrees of love are mandatory in diverse contexts, that is to say, there are a variety of love communities.

An example of a law that expresses an obligation within a love community is a piece of legislation enacted as soon as the contemporaneous Jewish state was founded. It is not a case of injustice if Jews are given special status in a "Law of Return" not granted to others. Any Jew who desires it may, by a simple declaration, after he establishes residence in the State of Israel, become a citizen; a privilege not extended to others. Justice, in the Jewish view, demands that special considerations obtain within a love community.

The second conception of merit that serves as a basis for the formulation of Jewish law is *moral* in character. Most of the obligations that the ideal of justice imposes on mankind derive not from the love, but from the moral, relationship. In addition to the *love community*, there exists a larger, *moral community* whose members uniformly possess the quality of humanity. Everyone born of human beings is himself a human being and is entitled to moral treatment. The human being is a moral being in a dual sense. He is a moral subject, that is, he is obligated, when he has the capacity to do so, to respond in a moral way towards others. He is a moral object, that is, he provides the occasion for others to perform moral acts in relation to him.

Here then is a sense of equality which encompasses all members of society. All men are equal in the sense that each is a moral object with respect to every moral subject. The prohibition on theft and murder is applicable not only to the favored group but to all human beings. Justice requires that these precepts guide our conduct equally with respect to citizen, stranger, and alien, adults, children, and infants. Nobody may be excluded from the company of those who are entitled to respect for their property and persons.[10]

In sum, there are two kinds of imperatives that are mandated by justice. One expresses the obligation to love another; the second expresses the need to respect his humanity. While it is difficult to define in precise terms these two categories of obligations, it may be said that, in general, in the case of interpersonal relationships, the obligations towards another that flow from his humanity take such forms as the need to repay a debt and the prohibitions on theft, murder, and adulterous relationships, while those that emerge out of love include, in addition, extending favors, assigning gifts, and advancing another's well-being.

Maimonides' formulation of the principle of equality in justice occurs in the context of his exposition of the law of theft and in connection with his description of the legitimate relationships of taxation that may occur between a monarch and his subjects. It is a law that is relevant to the moral community. The prohibition against theft is applicable to all, even to a sovereign. If the monarch or some other sovereign body were to single out any individual or group for special taxation, the targeted group would be the victim of injustice.

II

A few more observations are essential by way of clarifying the notion of universality as it enters into the concept of justice. First, the demand for universality is an ethical requirement. Many philosophers of ethics, notably Immanuel Kant, have argued that a maxim or a rule which, for whatever reason, cannot be universalized, is not a moral precept.[11] The rejection of any law as unjust on the grounds that it lacks the character of universality is tantamount to the subordination of political enactments to ethical principles. The requirement of universality is, in effect, the demand that the laws of society shall conform to moral imperatives.

Second, since justice should be embodied in the *application* of a law as well as in its *formulation*, the element of equality will have to be incorporated in both. The demand for procedural equality is made, for example, in the following biblical imperative, "Thou shalt not respect the person of the poor, nor favor the person of

the mighty, but in righteousness shalt thou judge thy neighbor."[12]
The jurist must apply a law to a particular case impartially, that
is, the social status of the defendant, for example, shall be irrelevant to the sentence or decision. But Judaism requires equality
in the statement of the law as well. Equality must characterize the
content of the law independently of the manner in which it is
applied. This is the essential focus of the dictum of Maimonides.

Third, Judaism does not require specific economic and social
standards by which rights and obligations have to be distributed
equally if the laws which assign these rights and obligations are
to be just. It recognizes the existence of a diversity of criteria, and
it acknowledges that a distribution may be regarded as consistent
with the requirements of equality and therefore just by one standard, though not by another. A graduated income tax law, for
example, may be perceived as assigning equal burdens by a standard of deprivations (the rich man who is taxed in a higher pro-
portion suffers approximately the same degree of deprivation as
does the poor man whose taxes are relatively small—though this
is clearly difficult to measure) while it imposes unequal burdens
by the standard of quantity (the wealthy contribute more to the
public coffers than do the poor). A sovereign or a legislative body
has the right not merely to enact a law but to choose the standard
with respect to which the justice of the law will be tested.

The talmudic principle enunciated by Samuel, "The law of the
land is the law,"[13] in effect, expresses this view. The talmudic sage
did not opt in favor of one over another type of political community. He recognized the possibility that justice may be based
on a variety of political ideologies. Irrespective of political philosophies, the essential criterion for the justice of a law is equality
by some standard.

This circumstance allows for the recognition that different
societies, organized in accordance with political principles associated with varying ideologies, may contain diverse systems of law
each of which may be just. Maimonides had no difficulty identifying as just a law promulgated by a single individual (the king)
in a monachial state so long as it assigns rights and obligations
equally. The laws enacted by a capitalistic society as well as those

legislated by a socialistic community may possess the character of justice. The standards with respect to which equality will be tested in such disparate political contexts will obviously differ. A socialistic society will insist on equality in the distribution of goods, for example, while its capitalistic counterpart will choose as its standard equality of opportunity. But so long as a law satisfies the requirement that, with respect to the selected standard, it distributes rights and obligations equally, it will be just.

Even in a single political context, a law which is just in one era may be unjust in the next. A political democracy is normally based on the theory of the social contract. It is entirely possible that a democratic community may agree to specific conditions for social cooperation in one generation and find them inadequate in the next. Twentieth-century America, for example, was not satisfied with the number of freedoms granted in the eighteenth and nineteenth centuries and demanded, in addition, freedom from want and fear. The implication of this demand is that it expected the enactment of legislation that would recognize the right of each citizen to be relieved equally of the pain of deprivation and the anxiety of fear. A law which violated these expectations might have been accepted as just in a past generation, but not today. The very concept of a contract, which presupposes an act of will by the members of a community, suggests that standards of justice are subject to change. If contractual acceptance is the ultimate basis for legitimacy in a democratic polity, it follows that a citizen's conception of what is socially acceptable may undergo transformation with the passing of time.

III

Universality, which we have interpreted as equality, is one of the essential elements in the Jewish conception of justice. Jewish law obligates us to treat equally those who, by relevant standards, are, as a matter of fact, equal. The ideal of justice is applied differently, on the Jewish view, to the love community and the moral community, but in both the formula of justice is identical: equality to those who are equal.

6

Justice and Consent

The consent of its members to the economic, legal, and political patterns that prevail in a democratic society is essential if it is to embody the ideal of justice. The notion of the social contract, which lies at the basis of democratic political theory, presupposes that a government cannot be just if it does not enjoy the consent of the governed. Any law or social procedure introduced without the approval of those to whom it will be applied cannot, in a democracy, lay claim to legitimacy. This is also true, at least in large measure, in the religious Jewish community. Granted that many principles and commandments by which the human being is governed may be construed as imposed—the seven Noachide commandments, for example—and yet as not violating the requirements of justice, the element of consent is, nevertheless, assigned a crucial and wide-ranging role in Jewish life. The imperatives of Torah were rendered obligatory upon the Jewish people by a voluntary gesture of acceptance. They became binding when the Jewish people adopted them in a gesture of covenantal commitment. Democratic patterns of designating community leaders prevailed in religious communities during large spans of Jewish history, and these involved the element of consent. Further, when Jews lived in the diaspora, they were required, in matters of civil law, according to the talmudic principle enunciated by Samuel, to abide by the law of the land; and this requirement had its source, according to some interpreters of this principle, in a gesture of consent.[1] It is essential therefore to clarify the manner in which the element of consent enters into the concept of justice.

A variety of questions must be addressed. Must consent be unqualified and wholehearted? Does the application of influence or pressure on an individual render his act of consent invalid? Can the consent of an elected representative be construed as an act of acceptance on the part of those who elected him? Is there a difference between the variety of consent demanded by Judaism and that required in a democracy? We turn to a clarification of the issues inherent in these questions.

I

In almost all cases, and with rare exceptions, acts of decision take place in an environment that tends to constrain the will. In the normal case, the human will acts in conformity with at least some of the forces to which it is exposed. Even when an individual abides by the precepts of morality and the prescriptions of Torah, he is acting in conformity with a tradition which was conveyed to him by training in the home, by education in schools, and by exposure to a religious environment. Such factors may readily be construed as interfering with the unconstrained action of his will. It is unreasonable and unrealistic to interpret the requirement of consent in terms of an action, entirely self-determined, which was not at all influenced by external forces. Consent cannot be characterized as a gesture occurring only in the absence of pressure.

What can be said—though, as we shall discover, this too is not entirely adequate—is that consent, when needed to render a transaction just, occurs when the agent performing the action does not experience the *sense* of being compelled. When an individual acts in circumstances in which he has no reservations with regard to the decision at which he has arrived, when all psychological factors relevant to his action support what he is determined to do, and none offers resistance, he may be said to be acting with wholehearted consent.

This is precisely the kind of consent that the rabbis of the

Talmud sought to associate with the Sinaitic gesture of commitment to the commandments. The conditions that prevailed at Sinai at the time the people of Israel was invited to accept the Torah were not conducive to an act of unqualified consent. Even according to the biblical account, the circumstances were such that the rejection of the commandments would have been virtually impossible. The children of Israel were surrounded by thunder and lightning, a thick cloud, and intimidating sounds of the shofar; the mountain trembled, and so did the people.[2] The rabbis perceived the coercive feature inherent in this event, and they embellished it to emphasize the point. "God picked up the mountain, placed it over their heads as if it were a barrel, and said to them, If you accept the Torah, well and good, if not, this will be your burial place." The sages then ask: if this is the case, the gesture of covenantal commitment was flawed; it was made under compulsion. They reply: notwithstanding, the Torah was accepted once again in the days of Ahasuerus, as it is written, "*kimu ve-kiblu ha-yehudim*," they reaffirmed that which they once accepted.[3] The reaffirmation, in appreciation of the miracle of Purim, was joyful, wholehearted, and without reservation.

It need hardly be stressed that the voluntary nature of the second gesture of acceptance in the days of Ahasuerus does not involve the absence of compulsion but rather the absence of the feeling, that is, the *sense*, of compulsion. Both Sinai and the event associated with Purim confronted the people of Israel with irresistible psychological forces. The difference was that while the former instilled fear, the latter inspired joy. At Sinai, the people felt themselves incapable of rejecting—they had a sense of their own terror and inability to act contrary to God's will. On the historic occasion connected with the celebration of Purim, they experienced gratitude and joy. They wanted to embrace God even if that meant the assumption of a whole range of obligations. The bridegroom, truly in love with his bride, joyfully places the ring on her finger notwithstanding the obligations that the act imposes upon him, and even while he is literally *driven* by his love, he has no *sense* of being compelled.

Hence, there need not be a correspondence between the feel-

ing of an individual that he is free of coercion and the reality
which may be such that existing conditions press him to act in the
way that he does. A person may believe that he is acting in total
freedom and in the absence of any constraints even while he is,
in fact, being pushed psychologically to undertake a certain course
of action. Notwithstanding, his act will be construed as voluntary
and the obligations as assumed willingly.

This variety of consent, however, is not always essential in the
talmudic perspective. There are circumstances in which, as the
Talmud puts it, "We apply force until he declares, 'I want to.' "[4]
This principle is applicable, for example, to a man who resists
divorcing his wife in circumstances when he is obligated to do so.
Granting a divorce must in all cases be a voluntary gesture. The
rabbis regard such a verbal declaration under conditions of coercion sufficient to confer upon his act of giving the divorce a voluntary character, though its performance is less than wholehearted.
Evidently, the *sense* of freedom from constraint is not demanded
in all instances in which consent is necessary. Consent admits of
degrees both as a psychological experience and as a legal gesture.

Apparently, the Talmud distinguished between an act of consent that is necessary for the *assumption* of obligations and one
that is called for when an obligation already exists and its *fulfillment*
requires that it be voluntary. At Sinai, the people of Israel was
called upon to *assume* obligations; hence, it was desirable that these
be undertaken wholeheartedly. If, on the other hand, the obligation exists already, as in the case of one who is required by
rabbinic decree to grant a divorce, it is sufficient that he declare
his desire, though his heart is not entirely in it. A Jewish court
has the right to introduce conditions that the husband would find
untenable should he continue to resist, conditions in which he
perceives it to be to his advantage to abide by the court's decision,
rather than to express his rebellious spirit.

To put this matter in another way, there are occasions when
to assume the presence of consent, it is sufficient that a person's
will respond affirmatively to an obligation, even while as a matter
of *inclination*, he resists it. The verbal declaration "I want to fulfill
my obligation" stated in conditions of coercion may be understood

as an expression of the *will* rather than the *emotions*. This declaration is the resultant of a variety of forces, some of which have their roots in the heart (hostility towards his wife, for example) and some in the understanding (the recognition that it is to his advantage to accede to the decision of the court; otherwise he will be subjected to intolerable economic sanctions). Even while the heart remains immersed in hostility, when coercion is applied, reason can counteract and overcome the inclination of the heart, leading the will to act in the best interest of the entire person. In circumstances where obligations already exist, it is not necessary to elicit an affirmative response from every component in the psychological anatomy of the personality; the voluntary expression of the will which represents the resultant of human faculties in conflict suffices. When obligations need to be assumed, however, as at Sinai, it is desirable that the whole individual—the heart, the mind, and the will—respond affirmatively.

Maimonides offers another interpretation of the meaning of consent in circumstances in which an obligatory act is resisted and where the element of compulsion is present. Where a Jew has an obligation to perform, even while he resists emotionally, the rabbis, according to Maimonides, estimated that in the depths of the recalcitrant personality there is a desire to comply but that he is prevented from doing so by powerful and overwhelming impulses. In such a context, one may conclude that consent exists even while the rod needs to be applied to compel him to articulate explicitly his readiness to conform. In a celebrated passage, Maimonides writes,

> Where the law requires that a man be compelled to divorce his wife [to give her a *get*], a Jewish court, in all places and at all times, may apply the lash until he says, "I want to conform." Why is this *get* not null and void? Because we do not describe an act as compelled unless a man was pushed and pressed to do something that he was not biblically obligated to do, as in the case where one is beaten until he sells his property or gives it away. But he whose evil inclination forced him to suspend a positive commandment or to commit a transgression and he

was beaten until he did that which he was obligated to do or refrained from doing that which was forbidden to him, then he is not to be regarded as compelled by the rod but by his evil thoughts. Therefore, he who does not wish to grant a divorce, since he wishes to remain within the Jewish community, to abide by the commandments, and to avoid transgressions, and it is his inclinations that overpowered him, and since he was beaten until his inclinations were weakened and he declared "I want to," his act of divorce is one performed with consent.[5]

On this interpretation too, an affirmative response from every faculty of the human personality is not essential to assure consent.

There is still another aspect to the element of consent that requires attention. It may be suggested that the reason that the talmudic sages sought to associate with the Sinaitic commitment a wholehearted response is that it was covenantal, that is to say, it was a one-sided, categorical, nonreciprocal commitment. I have argued elsewhere that the difference between a covenantal and a contractual commitment is that the former is categorical and absolute, and the latter hypothetical and conditional.[6] By means of a contract, A assumes a set of obligations to B only if B will fulfill certain undertakings towards A. A failure on the part of B to carry out his commitments implies that the conditional obligations A was prepared to assume do not take effect. A covenantal commitment, on the other hand, is one-sided and without conditions. Since the people of Israel at Sinai made a covenantal commitment, that is, there was no reciprocal gesture on the part of God, the rabbis determined it to be desirable that it be made without reservation. If, on the other hand, the assumption of obligation is contingent upon reciprocity, less than a wholehearted commitment might be sufficient. This appears to be the talmudic opinion.

If A compels B to sell him a parcel of real estate for fair value, and B complies because of coercion, there is a talmudic view that the sale is valid.[7] It is interesting to note that the Talmud supports this view by rational argument rather than by way of exegesis.

The grounds are, as one interpreter put it,[8] that the seller's desire to avoid the painful consequences of refusal together with the fact that he is being amply compensated suggest that the sale was indeed voluntary. In this instance too, the element of external compulsion is present; there is no real inclination to effect the transaction; the seller prefers to retain the parcel of land; there is no obligation to sell. Notwithstanding, because he received fair compensation, though he submits to the sale under compulsion, the transaction is legal. It appears, therefore, that only in the case of a covenantal commitment, where reciprocity is absent and unnecessary, is acceptance on the part of every component of the human personality essential. Where the seller receives payment, an affirmative response by the will suffices.

It is important to note that similar considerations are relevant to the assumption of political obligations. A political commitment is contractual, not covenantal. When a citizen accepts duties that citizenship in the state imposes upon him, he expects to receive something in return. Such circumstances allow for the validation of an act of consent that is not entirely wholehearted. This, according to some rabbinic interpreters, is the force of the principle "The law of the land is the law."[9] As one of them puts it, "All the members of the kingdom accept voluntarily the law of the king and his edicts and, therefore, the law is just; and if someone takes money belonging to another in conformity to the law of the sovereign, he is not guilty of theft."[10] Obviously, the individual who sustained a loss as a result of the application of this law is not happy about it. His surrendering of his material substance ought, however, to be regarded as an act performed with consent because, while he protests silently, he recognizes that his obedience to the law of the land is in his interests because of the benefits he accrues as a member of society.

II

It is evident from the discussion in the preceding section that consent need not always be wholehearted, even when it is needed to assure that a transaction to which it is a prerequisite is just. It should now be added that neither need consent always be explicit; perhaps not even conscious.

To begin with, when one assumes an obligation, it is not essential that he grasp all of its ramifications in order that his commitment shall be valid. If it were necessary to be fully conscious of the total meaning of the obligation that he assumes, that is to say, if he had to perceive all that was logically implied by his gesture, then few commitments would ever genuinely impose obligations, because it is not possible for the human mind to comprehend, at once, all that is contained in a proposition (which formulates a fact or an obligation) to which he gives his assent. A classic instance of this truth is provided by the realm of mathematics. In geometry, when one accepts The Euclidean axioms, he does not immediately perceive all that is logically implied by them. It may take a year, perhaps a few, of concentrated study to elicit all the implications of the fundamental propositions to which he gave his assent. The situation does not differ in the case of obligations. One does not normally grasp all the logical implications of the obligations which he adopts at the moment of commitment; it remains valid nevertheless.

A striking example of this is one interpretation of the Sinaitic commitment. According to the Talmud, and this has been noted already, the mountain was raised and held over the heads of the people of Israel, while they were warned of the dire consequences of their failure to accept the Torah. Again the question: if they were compelled, why was their commitment valid? Rabbi Joseph B. Soloveitchik offers a noteworthy interpretation:

> The action to which the Talmud refers was taken after the covenant had been voluntarily transacted on the preceding day. . . . It appears that God required two commitments on the part of the community: a general one to abide by the will of God while the community was still unaware of the nature of the commitment and a specific one concerning each individual law. The second commitment was assumed under constraint.[11]

It is noteworthy that a similar situation obtains in the case of a conversion. The would-be convert is required to make a commitment to God and Torah in the process of adopting his new faith. It is not, however, essential that he be fully aware of all the details of Torah at the time he takes this step. In the event that he persists in his intention to join the Jewish community notwithstanding the attempt to convince him that such a step is not necessarily conducive to the enjoyment of what is popularly perceived to be a pleasant life, the Code of Jewish Law declares that "we inform him of the fundamentals of the faith, which consists in the oneness of God and the prohibition of idolatry, and that we elaborate on this theme." Then we communicate to him "some easy commandments and some difficult commandments."[12] Accordingly, it is not necessary for the applicant for admission to the Jewish faith to be aware of all that he undertakes when he assumes the obligations of Torah, but he remains duty-bound to fulfill all of the obligations that follow from his general commitment, though he cannot be aware of them when he takes his step.

Further, there are circumstances in which consent exists even when a person is not aware that he is giving it. This occurs when those he has designated as his surrogates act in his behalf without his knowledge. The election process, in one form or another, has frequently been utilized in Jewish communities in the course of history. One well-known talmudic commentator declared that "the seven outstanding people in a city" whose consent the Talmud required in certain transactions,[13] are not seven people who distinguished themselves by way of wisdom, wealth, or prestige, but seven whom the community designated to serve as guardians of the affairs of the city.[14] When such people were elected to direct the life of the community, whatever they enacted had legal force. Their decisions were held to be equivalent to those taken by a majority of all the members of a community. The source of this authority was their designation as leaders and representatives by the community.[15]

It is evident that the election process presupposes an extraordinary conception of what constitutes consent. Citizens elect a number of individuals as their representatives, and implicit in such an election process is the declaration that those who cast ballots give their consent to all actions that will be taken by their representatives. Such consent is not nullified for an individual citizen should he reject a piece of legislation upon which his "consent" conferred legitimacy. This interpretation of "consent" is obviously indispensable in a *representative* democracy, that is, a state in which citizens elect a few from among themselves and assign to them the task of managing the affairs of the community. Judaism accepted the principle of representative consent. It grants that it is possible for an individual to give consent to a proposal of which he may be entirely ignorant, and that when such a proposal becomes law, it is incumbent upon him to obey it.

We may take this conclusion a step further. A citizen need not even vote to designate his representative. If the date and time of an election was publicized and he avoided participation, his inactivity and subsequent silence are again construed as an implicit declaration that he accepts the results of the election and consents to the subsequent legislative enactments of his representatives.[16]

III

A significant contrast can be drawn between the Jewish conception of the requirement of consent to justify the obligations to government and society and that demanded in a democratic context. On the Jewish view, "the law of the land is the law," according to most interpreters of this principle, because the Jewish citizen, in one form or another, consented to it. In a democratic society, it is also the case that the law of the land has validity because of consent—indeed, this appears to be a fundamental component of the social contract—but the two requirements of consent are not identical.

The consent demanded by the social contract is hypothetical and fictional. Advocates of the theory of the social contract do not claim or even remotely suggest that the social contract is an historic event, that is, that the members of a society assembled to consider the form of government to be adopted, and to give thought to the reciprocal obligations that should be assumed by citizens and government, in order to give their consent. Rather do they conceive of it as a theoretical experiment, an *imaginary* event in which citizens gathered to consider the parameters of government and to identify the social arrangement to which rational men would give their consent. Such arrangements are then construed as embodying the principle of justice. Consent in the context of the social contract then means, not that citizens in fact agreed to certain proposals, but that they would have agreed, if they had the opportunity to consider them in convention assembled and from a rational standpoint. The implication of this fact is that the gesture of consent is not really essential to the social contract; what *is* crucial is an understanding of the nature of men and an assessment of how rational individuals perceive their well-being. Presumably a rational citizen would consent to social arrangements which accord with his nature and are responsive to his self-interest, rationally considered.

John Rawls, a contemporary expositor of the theory of the social contract, for example, writes,

> I have assumed throughout that the persons in the original position are rational. In choosing between principles each tries as best as he can to advance his interests. . . . The concept of rationality invoked here . . . is the standard one familiar in social theory. Thus in the usual way, a rational person is thought to have a coherent set of preferences between the options open to him. He values these options according to how well they further his purposes; he follows the plan which will satisfy more of his desires rather than less, and which has the greater chance of being successfully executed.[17]

Such a theory is consistent with a conception which identifies rational self-interest as the ethical goal of man. If the social vocation of man is to seek and to achieve social arrangements which are genuinely advantageous to himself, then it is the objective existence of such arrangements rather than a subjective act of agreement that constitutes the essence of the just society. Since Judaism does not subscribe to a view that identifies the moral good with consideration of self-interest, because of its theological, that is, covenantal, orientation, it is not the self-interest embedded in social arrangements that guarantees their justice but the explicit, or even implicit, act of consent. The gesture of actual consent is an even more important component of the ideal of justice on the Jewish view than it is for American democracy.

7

Justice and Dissent

The practice of dissent is perceived as a virtue in American life. Whatever value, or lack of it, may attach to the opinion or conduct of the dissenter, the exercise of the right to dissent has, at least, this advantage: it is an act performed in freedom which, in itself, is highly prized in American society. Judaism does not see it just that way. A gesture of irresponsible dissent with perhaps destructive consequences has no value at all. The fact that it was, at the same time, an expression of freedom confers no merit upon it. One could not, for example, in Jewish terms, defend the speeches of Neo-Nazis on the grounds that in spewing anti-Semitic propaganda they are engaging in *acts* of freedom which deserve to be defended, irrespective of what they are saying, because of the intrinsic value of a free act.

Our concern will be with the political right of dissent. This should not be confused with the question that arises in a religious context. Whether a Jew has the right, according to Torah, to repudiate or to differ with a rabbinic opinion, authoritatively expressed—however the concept of authority may be understood—is one question; whether a citizen in the Jewish state or one who lives in the diaspora may dissent from decisions rendered by his government is quite another. It is the latter question that will command our attention.

Dissent may take either of two forms. One is speech—verbally or in written form, in private or in public. The other is disobedience—the nonviolent breaking of a law. An act of violence or the display of hostility when these are intended to express opposition to government will not be considered here, for such conduct raises other questions which will be discussed under the heading of revolution.

I

It is clear that Judaism condones and, in many instances, encourages dissent in the political arena. To cite a single, through central, rabbinic illustration, Maimonides declares,

> He who ignores a decree of the sovereign because he is engaged in the fulfillment of a commandment, even if the commandment is of lesser importance, bears no guilt; for, as between the commands of the teacher and the commands of his servant, the commands of the teacher are prior. It is certainly the case that when the sovereign's decrees suspend a commandment, he should not be obeyed.[1]

It must be stressed, however, that the Jewish justification of dissent is radically different from its American counterpart. In a democracy, dissent is a *right* that is derived from the *social contract*; in Judaism it is an *obligation* that is rooted in the *covenant*. The social contract is a political conception that stands at the foundation of the theory of democracy and states, in almost all of its interpretations, that citizens enter into a political association and assume obligations of obedience to law with the understanding that certain social conditions are fulfilled. When, as John Rawls puts it, "the conditions of social cooperation are not honored,"[2] a citizen has the right to engage in civil disobedience; that is, he has the right to dissent in action. The covenantal relation between the Jewish people and God, on the other hand, requires of the Jew that he assign a higher priority to covenantal than to political obligations. Should there arise a conflict between a man's duties to God and his obligations to society, he must submit to the former—even if that requires an act of political dissent.

II

An important consequence of the distinction between covenantal and contractual dissent is that the former is an obligatory response to social evil, no matter what its quantity or extent; while the latter would not be expressed unless the conclusion is reached that the evil in question is large enough to make dissent worthwhile by some utilitarian criterion. So Maimonides declared that a Jew should violate a precept of the sovereign even if the commandment which serves as the basis of his opposition is of lesser importance.[3] The covenantal Jew does not engage in *quantitative* calculations; he is concerned with the *quality* of the social phenomena. If, by religious standards, it is judged to be evil, it must be opposed. One does not dissent contractually, on the other hand, unless, as Rawls put it, the conditions of social cooperation are not honored, that is to say, as Rawls interprets it, the circumstances of social existence are not acceptable to the dissenter. The fact that a law is unjust does not provide sufficient grounds for opposition. Human society cannot attain ideal conditions. In the translation of the principle of justice into the laws of the land by means of constitutional procedures, inequities will inevitably emerge. In accepting the benefits of the institutions of democracy, an individual also assumes the obligation, Rawls claims, to abide by unjust laws as well. It is only when those laws enforce gross inequities or place oppressive burdens on segments of society, that is, when the conditions of social cooperation are not honored, that dissent in the form of civil disobedience is justified. In his words,

> In this way we become bound to follow unjust laws, not always, of course, but provided the injustice does not exceed certain limits. We recognize that we run the risk of suffering from the defects of one another's sense of justice; this burden we are prepared to carry as long as it is more or less evenly distributed or does not weigh too heavily. Justice binds us to a just constitution and the unjust laws which may be enacted under it in precisely the same way that it binds us to any other social arrangement. . . . And if in his judgment the enactments of

the majority exceed certain bounds of injustice, the citizen may consider civil disobedience.[4]

This view is unacceptable to Judaism, according to which, evil is not measured; it is merely opposed wherever and in whatever degree it may appear. The covenantal Jew cannot understand an obligation to accept injustice under any circumstances.

This difference between the contractual and the covenantal response derives from the circumstance that the former is a right and the latter an obligation. The *right* to dissent means that a citizen may exercise it if he is so inclined; he need not unless he finds it advantageous to do so. The pragmatic-utilitarian consideration is then the central factor to be taken into account. Since society is inevitably imperfect, a citizen would refuse to remain a party to a social contract only when the conditions of human existence are, from his point of view, unacceptable. If, however, the inclination to dissent is rooted in an *obligation*, the very perception of evil prompts opposition, no matter what its degree. It is conscience, not calculation, that is the basic factor.

The essential flaw in the contractual view, from the covenantal standpoint, is its justification of the *acceptance* of evil. In truth, social evils are accepted for a variety of reasons. Evil is generally recognized to be inevitable and unavoidable; therefore, there is widespread resignation to it. Man is afflicted with a sense of helplessness in the face of social patterns that wreak injustice on the weaker members of society, when it would require a massive force, normally not available to an individual, to change them. In such circumstances, social evils may be perceived but are ignored because of the judgment that what may be achieved is simply not worth the effort. There are still other psychological grounds for the acceptance of evil. After constant exposure to it, a person often becomes immune and insensitive to it. He fails to note the presence of darkness when he is unaccustomed to light. For example, an individual born into a society in which a specific group has been targeted for persecution often takes for granted, as a poet put it, that "whatever is, is right." One accepts social ills because he feels helpless to do anything about them; another because he fails to notice them. The theory of the social contract adds a third dimension to the acceptance of evil, namely, its justification. A citizen who made a contractual commitment, strangely enough, acquires an *obligation* to obey unjust laws. This conclusion is repugnant to the covenantal Jew.

In truth, covenantal dissent is an instrument for the *moral* transformation of society, while contractual dissent is merely a means of doing away with unacceptable *social* conditions. Dissent inspired by the social contract seeks to change existing institutions when these are unacceptable, so that they will the better conform to the citizen's conception of desirable social conditions. A covenantal act of dissent, on the other hand, seeks to instill a sense of moral commitment among the citizens of a political community. Even when it has, as an immediate objective, the transformation of an unjust institution, its ultimate purpose is to build moral personalities by exposure to moral institutions. Further, the covenantal personality engages in an ongoing struggle to bring society ever closer to the realization of the covenantal ideal. He can never rest in a state of untroubled satisfaction precisely because he knows that he lives in an imperfect world and he regards it as his vocation constantly to attempt to transform it. There is a fascinating rabbinic commentary which declares,

> When the righteous [*zaddikim*] wish to live at ease, the Holy One, blessed be He, says to them: "Are not the righteous satisfied with what is stored up for them in the world-to-come that they wish to live at ease in this world too?"[5]

The *zaddik* is a covenantal personality who feels himself driven to engage in a constant ongoing struggle within society to transform it in accordance with covenantal standards. There can be no peace for the *zaddik* in this world because he must always engage in dissent. Resignation to evil may be an acceptable political gesture; it cannot be tolerated as a covenantal response.

It follows that covenantal dissent is a more effective instrument of social progress than is its contractual equivalent. The person who recognizes that the acceptance of existing conditions in which evil is embodied, inevitable as evil may be in an imperfect world, is an abdication of responsibility and a repudiation of moral obligations will surely be prodded to undertake programs of social transformation more often and with greater eagerness than one who will not rock the boat when things are not too bad and who believes himself obligated to abide by unjust laws. But more of this later.

III

The contractual expression of dissent is limited by geographic boundaries which are irrelevant to its covenantal counterpart. There is nothing sacred about the "internal affairs" of a nation from the covenantal point of view. If my right is defined by an agreement with the members of a particular community, that is, a social contract, then the justification of opposition and disobedience flows from a violation of the agreement, and some natural impulse to choose that which will serve my interests. Once the contract is violated, I may rise in my own behalf, and what I do will normally be prompted by considerations of advantage. I have neither the obligation nor the desire to take risks for the sake of those beyond the boundaries of my own community. But such boundaries have no standing in the covenantal perspective. My obligation to act to remedy social ills is in force whenever they are perceived. I have a duty to respond in behalf of citizens beyond the boundaries of my own nation when their human rights are denied and when they are subjected to persecution. The prophet Jonah was instructed to proceed to Nineveh, a city to which he did not belong, to express dissent and opposition.

Accordingly, the contractual view attaches a legitimacy to the acceptance of evil in still another way. Not only is it sanctioned when it is relatively small; it may also be ignored when, though it is oppressive, it affects the citizens of a country to which the potential dissenter does not belong. Since inequities in a remote land have insignificant consequences for him, the contractually committed individual need not respond to them. It may be argued that such conditions do not generally exist, that no one in any part of the globe is really immune from the implications of oppression in any other part, that the progress of science and the advance of technology have made all people mutually interdependent —economically, socially, and politically—and that the concept of the social contract applies to the entire human family. Still, there is a difference between a conception of one world on the grounds that human destinies are everywhere reciprocally intertwined and one based on the view that we have a covenantal responsibility to oppose injustice wherever it may rear its ugly head. The former will rarely provide a basis for a sense of urgency to do something about evil that is intolerable to those beyond the boundaries of one's country.

IV

There is still another distinction between the two forms of dissent. Covenantal dissent is a response to the Infinite; contractual dissent is occasioned by the finite. To the religious mind, the obligation to oppose evil and injustice shares in the infinite dimension of its Source and calls for an infinite response. Such a response, how-ever, is not possible for a finite being, but in the attempt to relate to the Infinite, he feels impelled to strive for it nevertheless. This determination to achieve infinity in response (though impossible of realization) on the part of finite man is the essential charac-teristic of religious passion. Hence, covenantal dissent is accom-panied by a variety of passion to which the contractually inspired dissenter is a stranger.

One aspect of religious passion is self-abnegation. The reli-gious personality is largely indifferent to his own welfare when he is challenged by the Infinite; he is often prepared to make even the supreme sacrifice for the sake of His will. This is the significance of the talmudic principle *yehareg ve-al ya'avor*, that is, there are circumstances in which a Jew is obligated to lay down his life to sanctify the divine name. This is an element of religious passion which contrasts it sharply with its contractual analogue. The latter is normally motivated by self-affirmation (which also gives rise to a certain type of passion) rather than self-denial.

Another element in religious passion, and one to which reference has already been made, is the ongoing struggle to realize the ideal. It is not enough that social conditions be tolerable; they must also be consistent with covenantal principles. Since the ideal cannot be achieved—perfection is beyond human grasp—the covenantal personality can never rest. He is always engaged in the task of the moral transformation of society.

It is this kind of passion that confers power on religious dissent. To be sure, the contractual dissenter is also energized by passion, but it is a passion that has its source in the impulse to self-preservation and the desire for the good life. Its extent and, hence, its power, is circumscribed by human needs; it is motivated by finite considerations. Religious passion, on the other hand, is indifferent even to life and well-being, and those moved by it drive consistently, if not relentlessly, to the achievement of their goals. Indeed, its power cannot be measured.

It is true that religious passion must be contained within the bounds sanctioned by the Infinite; otherwise it manifests itself, not in religious zeal, but in fanaticism. The fanatic is one who is unable to choose appropriate means to achieve his aims, that is to say, his goals are not well served by his methods, which he also invests with religious passion. Alternatively, he is one who fails to understand that one infinite demand may be limited by another. For example, the obligation to observe the Sabbath may be suspended by another obligation to preserve life when it is threatened by illness. Religious passion, therefore, must be restrained by *rational* considerations, that is, by the thoughtful application of the principle of means and ends, and by the logical resolution of conflicts arising out of diverse infinite demands.

Religious passion needs also to be controlled by practical consideration of efficacy. It has been observed that passion can be prompted by self-serving as well as self-sacrificing motives. If passion is hypocritical, and thus is not prompted by a genuine sense of commitment, it will not often make an impact. If it is suspect, if it can be construed as not entirely honest, it will not make an impression. The sincerity of passion expressed in violence, in acts of vengeance, in the perpetration of vandalism is always in doubt; on the other hand, passion manifested in acts of self-sacrifice, in self-denial, will generally be viewed as deriving from genuine dedication and will inspire. Rabbi Akiva risking his life to study Torah is a more impressive model and a more effective paradigm of religious passion than the fanaticism of extremists who pour horror and destruction, ostensibly in the name of God, on those who do not agree with them. Religious passion must be restrained; but it remains a powerful instrument of social change nevertheless.

V

The covenantal personality reacts against immoral conditions but not against bad policies; the contractual personality dissents primarily against the latter.

This distinction is illuminating. It is possible that social policies may produce inequalities incompatible with the dissenter's conception of the social contract but consistent with the covenantal perspective. One cannot always predict the consequences of actions or the results of implementation of policies. It is conceivable that, well-intentioned though they may be, laws enacted by elected representatives, entirely in comformity with moral prescriptions and political objectives, will have unexpected consequences and may force segments of the community into poverty and hardship. The Torah anticipated and even predicted such developments, for which it prescribed a moral response, namely, charity to the afflicted. "For the poor shall never cease out of the land; therefore, I command thee, saying: Thou shalt surely open thy hand unto thy poor and needy brother in thy land."[6] To the covenantal thinker, such an arrangement, unacceptable though it may be on social grounds, does not violate moral or religious precepts and, hence, provides no basis for dissent. If the man of wealth made his substance available to the poor, the orphan, and the widow, he fulfilled his covenantal obligations. The contractual personality, on the other hand, may rebel against this state of affairs, for while it may not be immoral, he may perceive it as resulting from bad social policy.[7]

From the contractual point of view, the concept of a citizen's rights changes from one era to the next. In the American revolutionary war period, the social contract was regarded as a basis for the right to freedom of religion, press, speech, assembly, and the pursuit of happiness. Today it also serves as a ground for the demand for greater equality in the distribution of wealth, for the right to a job, a home, an education, medical treatment, and so on. It is not moral notions that have changed but political conceptions. Philanthropy is still a moral ideal, but citizens under the impact of the contractual view may be repelled by it and demand as a right that which heretofore could only be obtained by generosity.

It is possible that dissent against governmental decision may be prompted by either contractual or covenantal concerns, that is, as a matter of policy or religious principle. Citizens of Israel may object to the return of any part of Judea and Samaria to Arab sovereignty for reasons of policy (the loss of this land would threaten the security of the Jewish state) or out of religious considerations (Judea and Samaria are part of the Promised Land). American Jews, however, may on covenantal grounds join in the dissent (the covenantal commitment is independent of national boundaries), but not on contractual grounds (the contractual relation extends only to the parties to the contract). American Jews, therefore, do not have a legitimate basis for objecting to decisions of the Israeli government when they disagree merely as a matter of policy, that is, when they differ politically. They do have such a right if their dissent derives from a moral or religious commitment which they interpret in covenantal terms.[8]

VI

The act of dissent, for an American Jew with a covenantal perspective, is sanctioned politically and often required religiously. In expressing dissent, in word and in deed, he is, at times, expressing his membership in a contractual community but, more often, exhibiting his covenantal commitment. By means of dissent, he hopes to make a moral impact on human society.

8

Freedom

Freedom is both an American and a Jewish ideal. It is generally believed that the Jewish conception is identical to its American counterpart, so that in affirming their beliefs in freedom, American and Jew are articulating their commitments to the same principle. It is essential to note, therefore, that this is not the case. Important differences separate the two beliefs. They express in fact, two conceptions of freedom.

I

Freedom, in Jewish life, is a *national* goal; in the American perspective, it is an *individual* objective. It was the enslavement of the entire community of Israel that sparked the Jewish dream, and it was by means of the exodus that the *people* realized its hopes as a community. The right of the individual to deviate from established norms of belief and action is not included in the Jewish conception of freedom. The individual Jew is not granted the right to choose his beliefs; not even the right to worship God as he sees fit. "You shall not do after all that we do here this day, everyone whatsoever is right in his own eyes."[1] Nor is he permitted to deviate from rabbinic injunctions. "According to the Laws which they shall teach thee, and according to the judgment which they shall tell thee, thou shalt do; thou shalt not turn aside from the sentence which they shall declare unto thee, to the right hand, nor to the left."[2] *Sifrei* adds, by way of commentary, "Even if in your eyes they seem to tell you that right is left and left is right, listen to them."

It is true that the prescriptions for belief and action arising out of biblical precept and rabbinic interpretation do not preclude difference of opinion, variations in interpretation, and the expression of individuality. It is probable that talmudic methodology implies that debate is to be encouraged in those areas where behavior is not altogether controlled by rabbinic decision. There remains, on the Jewish view, a large class of principles and precepts about which controversy was, to say the least, discouraged. In short, Judaism does seek uniformity in commitment and behavior within the Jewish community. Its goal is a unity through homogeneity, not a unity of diversity. And this striving for uniformity is not regarded as inconsistent with its emphasis on freedom.

Included in the American political objective, however, is freedom for each individual as well. The individual has the right of choice. His view may be entirely mistaken. His actions may be detrimental to his own well-being. So long as he does not interfere with the rights of others to do that which they regard as in their interests, he may not, if freedom is the rule, be compelled to act contrary to what he believes to be his own. In other words, freedom also means that an individual has the right to be wrong. John Stuart Mill gave the classic expression to this demand in his work *On Liberty*. In regard to the right of belief Mill writes, "If all mankind minus one, were of one opinion, and only one person were of the contrary opinion, mankind would be no more justified in silencing that one person, than he, if he had the power, would be justified in silencing mankind."[3] The liberty of action is obviously not so extensive; but it is limited only by the rights of others—which may not be interfered with—to strive for the achievement of what they identify as desirable. As Mill puts it, "The only freedom which deserves the name is that of pursuing our own good in our own way, so long as we do not attempt to deprive others of theirs, or impede their efforts to obtain it."[4]

This distinction between the two interpretations of the ideal of freedom is not arbitrary or accidental; it follows from a difference in the American and Jewish conceptions of their ultimate purposes. Essentially, the goal of a democracy is to guarantee to every person the right to pursue the good life according to his own formula. The intent of religion, on the other hand, is to describe a specific notion of the good life, to exhibit the means of attaining it, and to inspire the adoption of its program. Democracy, in its American form, for example, was established to provide a system that could serve as the basis of a pluralistic society. The architects of the American political structure were therefore more concerned with the *right* to pursue happiness than with its delineation and distribution among all citizens. To have legislated the contents of this ideal and its imposition on all would have had as a concomitant effect the repudiation of that very right which was America's primary and paramount concern. The main thrust of religion, on the other hand, is the communication of an idea that will inspire single-minded commitment and the rejection of the alternatives available in a pluralistic society.

It may perhaps also be worth noting in this connection that the concept of individual liberty as a political objective is of recent vintage. Isaiah Berlin in *Two Concepts of Liberty* writes,

There seems to be scarcely any discussion of individual liberty as a conscious political ideal (as opposed to its actual existence) in the ancient world. Condorcet had already remarked that the notion of individual rights was absent from the legal conceptions of the Romans and Greeks; this seems to hold equally of the Jewish, Chinese, and all other ancient civilization that have since come to light.[5]

This distinction in the two conceptions has an important corollary. The American notion of freedom requires *independence*, that is, self-determination; the Jewish idea associates freedom with the state of *dependence*. The right of independence—for individual as well as nation—is essentially alien to the Jewish perspective.

What is regarded as central to life in freedom, on the American view, is that the will of each individual—which may very well be quite arbitrary—determine the course that he will follow. The ideal instance, the free personality in a paradigmatic sense, is one whose every act of will is followed by corresponding behavior. All restraints—physical, biological, psychological, social—impinge upon and limit the freedom of man. If the human being cannot roam at will among the stars; if he cannot live in the emptiness of space; if he must abide by the law of the land, to that extent, he is deprived of liberty—for he must frequently behave in a manner that is contrary to his own volition. The ultimate in this variety of freedom, according to one philosopher, can be attributed to the Divine Being and to Him alone. He wrote, "That thing is called free which exists from the necessity of its own nature and *is determined to action by itself alone*," and concluded, "God alone is a free cause."[6] Through the identification of freedom with independence or self-determination, the human will is elevated to the highest level of importance, considerations of truth and morality are subordinated to it, and the individual is transformed into a legislator of ethical doctrine.

Judaism opposes the assignment of such primacy to the will. It objects to the subordination of classic religious values to what are frequently arbitrary and unreasoned acts of volition. The Jew understands the principle of the centrality of the will in purely pragmatic political terms. It is precisely under a government organized according to this principle that he can live his religious commitment without interference. Still, this type of freedom is merely a practical necessity. In absolute terms, he must submit to truth and moral precepts, that is, the will of God. This, I take it, is the essential meaning of the rabbinic lesson, "For none can be considered free except those who occupy themselves with the study of the Torah."[7] The free individual is dependent on the divine will.

It is because of this fact that the religious personality is distressed when the notion of freedom is pushed to the point where it is taken as a justification of every random moral decision. In the classic perspective, a person must estimate the morality of any act he is about to perform in the light of a moral code that is regarded as objective and universal. The new morality, emerging as it does out of a matrix of freedom which makes the free man morally self-determined, turns every individual into the legitimate author of his own moral doctrine and the exclusive judge of his own moral action.[8] The arbitrary will has thus become the sacred will. For the Jew, the arbitrary will is, at best, not very useful and, at worst, a harmful instrument.

II

There is another fundamental distinction. According to the American conception, freedom denotes a *right*. On the Jewish view, it refers mainly to a *power*.

The exodus is the historical event that serves as the basis for the Jewish celebration of freedom. It should be stressed that the exodus is a fact, not a norm. It is an event, not a covenant. It made available to the ancient Hebrews the *power* of choice, not the *right*. The Jewish people was deprived of a power during the period of its enslavement which it regained upon its departure from Egypt. At Sinai, the people received norms and obligations, not rights—except in a secondary sense. Hence it is not the right but the power to choose that constitutes the essential ingredient in the Jewish conception of freedom.

Judaism's denigration of rights in the characterization of its conception of freedom is a direct consequence of its supreme concern with *duties* or *obligations*. It has been noted that rights and duties are correlative; that is, "right" is defined in terms of a limitation on duties, and "duty" is defined in terms of a limitation on rights. As one philosopher put it.

We may assume that "right" and "duty" are correlative terms: A man has a right to perform a certain act A if, and only if, it is not his duty to refrain from performing A; and he has a duty to perform A if, and only if, he does not have the right to refrain from performing A.[9]

Hence emphasis on the rights of an individual is necessarily accompanied by a restriction of the domain of his obligations; while stress on obligations involves a concomitant limitation in the area of rights.

Judaism's paramount concern is with the imposition of obligations, that is, *mitzvot*. Their commanding authority derives either from the rightness of the act prescribed by the imperative (which should be construed in religious terms as the expression of the divine will) or from the rightness of the act together with the fact of commitment. The Noachide commandments are universal obligations. They do not presuppose a covenant or an act of acceptance. Everyone in the human family is duty-bound to abide by them. The other *mitzvot* of Torah, expressive of the divine will though they may be, do not impose obligations until they are accepted by covenant. Once, however, the people performs its act of commitment, the obligation takes effect for all who are born into the covenantal community. Of course, where obligations have not been formulated, where duties have not been prescribed, and where the possibility of choosing incompatible courses of action exists, the right of choice remains.

The *power* to choose, on the other hand, is essential to the Jewish conception of freedom for two reasons. First, an act of commitment cannot be performed in a state of coercion. If the Jew's obligation to comply with *mitzvot* rests, at least in part, on the fact of a covenant voluntarily accepted by the people of Israel, then there can be no obligation if there is no power to accept. The primary significance of the exodus is that it was an essential prerequisite to the act of commitment that took place at Sinai.

Second, there is no morality without the power to choose.[10] An individual may be held morally accountable for the violation of a moral precept, not to steal, for example, if he had the power to do otherwise. In a state of slavery, where his life is not his own and is always in jeopardy when disobedient, the slave does not have the power to refuse compliance; hence his act of theft cannot be construed as immoral.

It should be noted, by way of anticipating possible objections, that the American conception of freedom, while emphasizing the right of choice as its central ingredient, does not necessarily exclude the element of power. The current debate as to whether American society is indeed free turns on the prior question as to whether an individual who has the right of choice without the power is really free. No one denies the fact that the American legal system grants to each the right of choice. But there are those who ask: of what value is such a right if it is not accompanied by the necessary power? Can a society which legally confers a right be regarded as free if, at the same time, its very structure prevents some of its citizens from exercising that right? Hence, there are those who add the element of power to that of right in defining the American conception of freedom.[11] Notwithstanding, it is the element of right which is central to the definition. Power is needed to make the right meaningful. According to the Jewish conception, it is the element of power that is paramount.

There is another way of putting this. It is popular among social thinkers to distinguish between "freedom from" and "freedom of." "Freedom of" refers to a right. Freedom *of* speech, *of* press, *of* religion denote the right to speak, publish, and preach according to one's conceptions and commitments. "Freedom from" refers to a power. To achieve freedom *from* want, *from* fear, *from* ignorance, *from* enslavement is to succeed in removing the obstacles that stand in the way of choosing a desirable pattern of living. Judaism's emphasis is on freedom *from* because its purpose is to guarantee the power to choose. In fact, so much of biblical history and legislation is concerned with establishing just this power. The exodus contributed to power by removing the shackles of human slavery. The Sabbath increases human power by removing the chains that prevent man from rising above the economic struggle. Social legislation adds to power by lifting from the human being the constraints of poverty. Study adds to power by liberating man from the errors due to ignorance. Judaism is clearly concerned with freedom—not freedom *of* but freedom *from*. The American conception, on the other hand, begins with the idea denoted by "freedom of." The Constitution guaranteed the right of choice. This concept of freedom was expanded only recently to include the element of power in the demands for freedoms *from*.

III

There is still another important distinction that should be drawn. Freedom is an *end* of political democracy. It is a *purpose* of the American form of government to guarantee life in freedom. Judaism's goal, however, is the embodiment within the community of a certain way of life. Freedom is merely a *means* to that end.

This distinction implies that to attain freedom's objective, on the American view, it is necessary to *multiply opportunities* and at least to *preserve a variety of possible commitments*. If freedom means the right to choose, the wider the range of choice, the greater the freedom. When construed as a goal, freedom is not static. It grows when the frontiers of possible action are pushed out. A person who must select one of two possibilities is not as free as one who is presented with the choice of a dozen. An individual who by virtue of education and social position is a candidate for a variety of professional and vocational positions has more freedom than one whose opportunities are limited because he has been deprived. Those who are charged with the task of expanding freedom are engaged in an enterprise that is never completed. New methods of education always emerge; new opportunities, in all fields of endeavor, are always introduced; novel ideas making a claim to human commitment always appear. Those who value freedom in its American form welcome this variety with enthusiasm. Furthermore, freedom was born on American shores principally to guarantee the possibility of a multiplicity of commitments. The architects of the American form of government insisted that people with conflicting claims and incompatible religious commitments can form a unified nation. Judaism, on the other hand, requires freedom not to preserve or increase the varieties of possible experience, but to enrich life by the introduction, in an ever growing sphere and in a more meaningful way, of the one Jewish experience. Hence, while it will undoubtedly confer its blessings on any enterprise that will serve to expand economic and social opportunities, it will not regard such pursuits as exemplifications of its major concern. It will, on the other hand, repudiate the notion that its conception of freedom guarantees to each individual the right to choose one of a variety of incompatible religious creeds.

This distinction supplies the reason why certain problems arise in the application of the American conception of freedom which do not appear in the implementation of its Jewish counterpart. The first of these has to do with excluded possibilities. Given that multiplicity of commitment should be preserved in a state of freedom, are there some varieties that should be proscribed? This question comes to the fore in both the political and the moral domain.

First, the political arena! The Bill of Rights guarantees the freedom of the spoken and written word. It thereby encourages the introduction into the American experience of a variety of incompatible political views. Does it also guarantee the right to discuss and teach a political doctrine which, if implemented, would destroy the system which allows it? Does democracy, for example, provide the right to urge the acceptance of a form of totalitarianism which is inconsistent with democracy? Many insist on an affirmative reply. Insofar as speech is concerned, if consequences seriously inimical to the democratic process are not clear and present, the freedom to speak may not be restrained.[12] So important is democracy's task of retaining a multiplicity of possibilities that many judge it desirable to endure a suggestion that must be regarded as evil—at least in a democratic context—in order to assure the unhampered introduction of a variety of ideas that are useful. Could an analogous question ever arise in the interpretation of freedom in the context of Judaism? Surely, no one would suggest that, in endorsing the ideal of freedom, Judaism provides the right to teach and to urge in its sanctuary a doctrine which, if adopted, would spell the destruction of Jewish life. No one expects Judaism to be so tolerant as to permit the preaching of Christianity, for example, from a synagogue pulpit. The reason is clear. Judaism, like Christianity or any other religious creed, is concerned not with increasing the *variety* of religious experience but with the introduction and propagation of *one* religious experience.

A similar difference in response arises in connection with commitments of a moral sort. Judaism's negative reaction to the phenomenon of pornography on stage and screen is clear and explicit. Its acceptance of freedom provides no basis for the justification of activities which, by its own criteria, are immoral. For the American, however, the task of preserving a multiplicity of moral creeds points inevitably to the problem of circumscribing the domain of acceptable moralities. And the grounds for removing pornography from American life must be sought in the "clear and present" threat that it poses to the survival of American society and not in the fact that it is incompatible with one or another of the classic religions.

Another question that arises in connection with the application of the American conception of freedom has to do with the extent to which a democracy should go in ensuring the preservation of plurality. Should a democratic government adopt a policy of *laissez-faire* in the hope that, in the normal course of events, varieties of political views, religious doctrines, and moral creeds will be preserved? Or, should government actively channel and direct events to guarantee that pluralism of various forms will be maintained? The answer to this question is relevant to the issue of federal aid to religious education. Setting aside, for the moment, other related considerations, constitutional, economic, and so on, it does seem to be a fact that, in providing such aid, government is helping to preserve pluralism in religious creeds, the very type of pluralism that is so essential to freedom.

It could be argued, for example, and I believe with cogency, that the *laissez-faire* attitude was appropriate to the eighteenth and nineteenth centuries, but that currently, with the unrestrained technological thrust towards uniformity, and with the revolution in communications media which renders every home easy prey to their enormous homogenizing influence, a deliberate effort on the part of government to preserve plurality, by way of federal aid, for example, would be in order. But Judaism's support for this program is, at best, problematic. In endorsing it, the Jew is also demanding assistance for religions whose creeds include a variety of principles that contradict his own, and which, at least historically, regarded the Jewish community as a major target of missionary activity. Hence, neither of the available alternatives on this issue is, to him, wholly satisfactory. As an American committed to freedom, an individual can respond readily and enthusiastically in support of federal aid. As a Jew, he may have reservations.

IV

Let it not be supposed that because the two conceptions of freedom differ, Judaism and democracy are incompatible. On the contrary, they are complementary. Democracy presupposes the existence of various philosophies of life, which can function in a way that it, by virtue of its very nature, cannot. The different religions express just such philosophies.

Democracy assumes that (1) every member of society has the right to choose that which he desires and to act according to his choice; and (2) given a certain amount of education, a human being can, in most instances, choose intelligently among alternatives. Democracy does not assume that (3) every human being can, even after extensive study, construct out of his own imagination a theory of human happiness that will bring him, should he guide himself by it, the satisfaction he seeks. Various theories must be presented to him. From a political vantage point, this is precisely the major function of religion in a democratic society.

9

Individualism

A great deal of importance is placed on the individual in both the theory of democracy and in Jewish thought—and with good reason. The great achievements of mankind are not generally due to the effort and the vision of a multitude but to the creative activity of individuals working alone or, at times, in collaboration with a few others on a single project. Throughout history it has been *individuals* who have uncovered the mysteries of the universe, *individuals* who have produced the great masterpieces of literature and art, *individuals* who have emerged as prophetic personalities or as moral heroes. The principle of majority rule is essential to the preservation of political arrangements which we believe are the best available to mankind; but it does not function as a guide to creativity or progress. It is little wonder that the portion of mankind that has placed a premium on creativity and progress has assigned the highest value to individuality.

But Judaism stresses the importance of the individual for still another reason, namely, that each human being is held to have been created in the image of God—and this is a doctrine not normally included in theories of democracy. The fact that a divine element somehow inheres in man attaches to him an importance that even a multitude may not be able to erase.

The individualism that Judaism advocates is multifaceted: (1) it urges heroism in the fulfillment of *obligations* rather than in the

104

exercise of *rights*; (2) it often assigns an importance to the individual as great as that which it associates with the community, because of the *value* inherent in personality; and (3) it encourages intellectual opposition, even while it insists on obedience, to authority.

I

Individualism, on the Jewish view and in the first place, means resistance on the part of the individual to pressures exerted upon him by the multitude. It means this in a democratic context as well, but democracy insists on what is, for it, a more basic variety of individualism, one which Judaism rejects, namely, the right of a person to do as he pleases so long as another is not harmed in the process. This variety of individualism is, in effect, identical with freedom. Indeed, freedom and the individualism of rights are closely intertwined. Political thinkers who advocate and elaborate on the concept of freedom invariably affirm an individualism of rights. The English philosopher Mill devoted his entire classic *On Liberty* to mapping out the vast domain in which an individual may do as he pleases, that is, the domain of rights, and he applauded the man, that is, the individualist, who insists on doing so. Judaism, however, because it opts in favor of an individualism of obligations, does not attach to it a concern for freedom.

But Judaism and democracy agree that individualism means a determination to live by one's commitments. That determination may derive from a belief, American style, that the right to act on inclination is worth fighting for, or it may be inspired by the Jewish conviction that a Jew is obligated to behave in accordance with the precepts of Torah. In either case, he who believes in individualism will defend his right or fulfill his obligation even if it requires resisting the majority. Mill, who advocated individualism as a political doctrine, expressed this view in the demand that citizens shall have the right and the capacity to resist "the tyranny of the majority."[1] It is not necessary to go along with a popular consensus unless one is convinced that it reflects his personal views.

Judaism does not accept an individualism of rights; it does not allow the view that each person has the right to act on impulse or inclination, irrespective of whether such tendencies conform to obligations prescribed by the Torah. One example is associated with worship in ancient days: the ancient Jew was prohibited from offering sacrifices in a location other than the Holy Temple in Jerusalem. The Bible declares, "You shall not do after all that we do here this day, everyone whatsoever is right in his eyes."[2] Of course, when faced with an option with respect to which Judaism offers no guidance, an individual has complete freedom of choice,[3] but we would not characterize a doctrine that confines the domain of liberty to making innocuous decisions as advocating an individualism of rights. The latter variety of individualism sanctions opposition to fundamental principles of political as well as moral and religious systems.

But Judaism does advocate an individualism of obligations. There are three laws that a Jew is not permitted to violate under any circumstances, no matter what the threat to life and well-being. These are the prohibitions on idolatry, adultery, and murder. In times of *shemad*, when hostile governments proscribe Jewish observance of any kind with the explicit intent to eradicate Jewish life, the Jew is obligated to defend, with his life, all precepts of Torah.[4] In addition, should a Jew live in an alien political environment in which legislation is enacted contrary to Torah obligations, where the intent, however, is not to subvert Judaism, and where his life is not endangered, it is still his duty to disobey.[5] In Jewish life, such responses constitute individualism *par excellence*, but they represent an individualism of obligations.

Our main task, then, is to draw the consequences of the doctrine that advocates this kind of individualism and to distinguish it from that which endorses an individualism of rights. One major aspect of the Jewish variety of individualism is that it generally involves the posture of self-denial rather than self-assertion. The declaration of the American patriot, "Give me liberty or give me death," expresses both individualism and self-assertion. He declared his intention to resist all efforts to deny him freedom, no matter what the consequences (individualism), but he was prepared to do this to secure freedom for himself (self-assertion). His goal was "Give me liberty." This is the kind of individualism that is normally associated with the advocacy of rights. Jewish individualism involves self-denial; it is normally manifested in acts of unselfishness and self-sacrifice. It is the individualism of obligation.

Unlike the individualism of obligations, the individualism of rights is paradoxical. The very essence of the posture of individualism is the willingness to experience pain and suffering in order to accomplish a valued purpose. The individualistic gesture is then associated with an attitude of indifference to the self. But when this courageous stance is adopted to secure a condition that is personally advantageous, the inherent selflessness of individualism is combined with and subordinated to a self-interested goal. In the case of the individualism of obligations, on the other hand, both the courageous gesture and the goal are equally unselfish.

Clearly, the posture of individualism requires the manifestation of strength of purpose; but such strength increases and is rendered more lasting when the purpose is not selfish. This accounts for the incredible determination of the Jew to survive the many trials that confronted him in the course of his turbulent history and his spectacular success in doing so. It accounts too for the historic resistance, on the part of the Jew, to the forces of assimilation. Remaining impervious to ideological storms and winds of doctrine in a pluralistic society is no easy undertaking for a community that constitutes a very small minority of a population. That the Jewish people was able to do this, notwithstanding varying degrees of erosion in the diverse societies in which it found itself, is a result of the power inherent in an individualism of obligation.

Further, individualism *par excellence* is manifested in the personality of the hero. However, the two varieties of individualism provide, in effect, the basis for the cultivation of two types of heroes. The heroic advocate of the individualism of rights manifests extraordinary courage on the field of battle. There is glory to be gained, and the hero rejoices in it. The battlefield makes available an outstanding opportunity for self-assertion. The heroic representative of an individualism of obligations, on the other hand, characteristically displays his power unnoticed and removed from the public eye, in a context in which glory, fame, and the applause of the multitude are not available. He does not seek an opportunity for self-affirmation. It is significant to note that the Jewish historical model of the hero is not the one who fights valiantly on the field of battle but he who successfully, sometimes even with his life, opposes the forces intended to remove him from patterns of Jewish living.

In truth, the Jewish concept of the hero is to be distinguished not only from its counterpart in the democratic version, but from the general idea of the hero. When this idea is elaborated even in independence of considerations of freedom, the element of self-affirmation is generally included. On one totalitarian view, for example, the hero, or, to use the terminology of the philosopher in question, the world-historical individual, is moved by the spirit of the age; notwithstanding, "These world-historical men also satisfy themselves."[6] The kind of satisfaction that they enjoy is derived from fulfilled self-interest.

> We assert that nothing has been accomplished without an interest on the part of those who brought it about. And if "interest" be called "passion" . . . we may affirm without qualification that *nothing great in the world* has been accomplished without passion.[7]

While Judaism will, no doubt, grant that the hero is moved by passion, it perceives such passion as motivated, not by the demand for rights or considerations of self-interest, but by a commitment to a transcendent purpose.

II

Another form of individualism that is central to Jewish thought is that which holds that the life of an individual cannot, in general, be sacrificed for that of the community. The classic Jewish statement of this principle is well known.

If idolators said to them [a group of Jews]: Give us one from among you that we may kill him, and if you refuse, we shall kill all of you, let them kill every one, but let not one Jewish soul be surrendered to them.[8]

Neither an explicit choice of one individual as a sacrifice nor the casting of lots is allowed as a means of saving the community. Nor does it matter whether the group consists of a handful or is large in number.[9] Further, even if the enemy designates a particular individual and demands that he be surrendered if the remainder of the community is to be saved, there is one view, and Maimonides takes it to be authoritative, that this may not be done unless the individual in question did something that made him deserving of death.[10] Clearly, there are circumstances in which it may be said that, from the standpoint of Judaism, the life of a single individual is equal in value to the lives of all in a community.

The rationale for this view derives from several considerations. First, in view of the fact that every human being is held to have been created in the image of God, each person's humanity possesses infinite value. It is at least part of the definition of that which is infinite that the sum of several things that are infinite in quantity is not greater than one infinite quantity. In fact, this is the essential element in the definition of *infinite* in mathematics. As one philosopher put it:

The maxim in question is, that if one collection is part of another, the one which is part has fewer terms than the one of which it is a part. This maxim is true of finite numbers. . . . But when we come to infinite numbers, this is no longer true. This breakdown of the maxim gives us the precise definition of infinity. A collection of terms is infinite when it contains as parts other collections which have just as many terms as it has.[11]

Of course, in mathematics, we deal with infinite *quantity*, while human life is measured in terms of infinite *value*. It is not unreasonable, however, to assume that the definition of infinity in the case of quantity is applicable equally in the case of value.

To say, therefore, that the life of each human being is of infinite value is to say more than that all men are equal. If all men are equal, it could be cogently argued that one human being is equal to another but that two human beings are of greater value than one. If the life of a single individual is of infinite value, however, then his life is equal in value to the life of an entire community.

There is a second factor that lends support to the equation which identifies the value of the life of an individual with that of the community, namely, every individual is himself a potential community. As the Talmud puts it, "He who saves the life of a Jew is credited with saving the life of an entire world."[12] The individual is potentially the ancestor of a multitude. It is in this sense that God, in his promise to Abraham, declared, "I will make you into a large nation."[13] An equivalence is suggested in this verse between Abraham (the individual) and "a large nation." Since, biologically speaking, the life of an individual continues, even following his death, in the lives of his descendants, the equivalence has a certain literal validity. It follows that we cannot undertake to measure, even quantitatively, the life of an individual; it may indeed be unlimited, even in temporal dimension.

There is still another consideration that deserves attention. In Jewish thought, there is a certain mathematical dependence between the value of a human personality and the obligations that are his to perform; that is, the more numerous the obligations, the greater his value. The higher value of a Jewish life derives from the fact that the Jew has 613 imperatives to obey. Within the Jewish community, those charged with increased obligations occupy a higher status. The greater importance of the *kohen* (priest), for example, is reflected in the role that he occupies in the performance of added rituals in Jewish life.

If this is granted, there is still another reason for equating the value of a single Jewish life to that of a community, namely, that the obligations imposed on every individual member of the Jewish community consist of no less than the obligations imposed on the entire Jewish community. As the rabbis of the Talmud put it, "All

Jews are responsible one for another,"[14] an observation that is further explained to mean, based on an interpretation of a relevant biblical passage, that each Jew is subject to punishment for the transgressions of all his fellow Jews. Thus, from a halakhic, that is, legal, standpoint the obligations carried by a single Jew are equal, quantitatively, to the sum total of the obligations of all Jews. In a very significant sense, each Jew is entitled, and perhaps obligated, to say, "I am the Jewish community." There is then a legal equation that identifies the value of personality with community.

There is a final consideration which may be worth mentioning. Judaism adopts what may be regarded as an organic conception of Jewish community. This means that this community is not a collectivity which includes a multiplicity of individuals, each of whom is essentially independent of the other; it is rather an organism to which each individual belongs as an indispensable part. In this perspective, it can be suggested that the life of the community depends on the life of each Jew, and, accordingly, that the value of the latter is commensurate with that of the former.

In any case, these attitudes, underscored in Jewish thought, adumbrate the position that individualism, in the Jewish perspective, far from maintaining the independence of each person from others, expresses rather the kind of interdependence that contributes meaning to the view that the value of individual life is equal to that of the community.

III

Judaism is also very much aware of the potential for creativity that inheres in still another variety of individualism, namely, the intellectual opposition to authority. Two things need to be stressed in this connection. First, intellectual opposition is not unexceptionally permitted. There are contexts in which it is proscribed. On one view in the *Code of Jewish Law*, a student may not disagree with his teacher of Torah, even when he can prove, by reference to rabbinic sources, that his teacher is mistaken;[15] he may not even render a decision on Torah questions, assuming he is competent to do so, without authorization from his Torah teacher.[16] One aspect of the modern institution of *semikhah*, ordination, is that, by its means, the rabbi who is the teacher of Torah authorizes his student to render decisions on questions of Jewish law even during his (the teacher's) lifetime. Further, the biblical obligation to fear a parent is interpreted to mean, among other things, that a child is not allowed to contradict his parents.[17] But freedom to disagree is granted beyond such limitations.

Secondly, while there is extensive liberty to disagree, there is little freedom to disobey. If a great sage, on the basis of extensive scholarship and deep understanding, decided that a decision of the Sanhedrin, the most authoritative body in Jewish life, was in error, he placed his life in jeopardy if he acted contrary to its decision.[18] He was permitted to articulate his opposition but not to put his own views into practice.

This arrangement, that is, the freedom to disagree combined with the obligation to obey, invested Judaism with internal strength and the potential for extraordinary creativity. Contrary to what many believe, Judaism did not advocate a diversity of practice in Jewish life. While it assigned a great deal of value to unity in diversity in the intellectual arena, it did not endorse this as an ideal in the realm of conduct. It appeared to many Jewish thinkers that a uniformity of practice was a desideratum of Jewish life. Here is one expression of this view:

And this commandment [to abide, without deviation, to the decisions of the Sanhedrin] was exceedingly necessary because the Torah was given to us in written form, and it is well known that there will not be general agreement with respect to novel situations, and disagreements will multiply, and the Torah will become many Torahs; therefore the decision was biblically rendered that we shall obey the Great Sanhedrin which is located in the presence of God in the place which He chose [the Holy Temple in Jerusalem] in all that it will instruct us in regard to the interpretation of Torah—whether the interpretation was received, witness from witness, reaching to Moses our teacher, who received it from God, or was offered on the basis of the meaning of the Torah and its intent.[19]

It is clear from the biblical context in which this interpretation is offered that the rejection of circumstances that could be described as "many Torahs" refers to the existence of different patterns of conduct rather than the occurrence of different theoretical perspectives. It is true that not all questions reached the Sanhedrin, so that even when that ancient body existed, variations in practice may well have prevailed in the Jewish community. Notwithstanding, the conclusion that such diversity was always an ideal of Torah is, to say the least, unwarranted.

Theoretical diversity, on the other hand, was always a Jewish ideal because it served to enrich Jewish life and to enhance Jewish creativity. The classic and, by far, the best-known talmudic statement that endorses and idealizes differences in interpretation of Torah is the one which, commenting on the frequent disagreement of the schools of Shammai and Hillel, declares, "The opinions of both are the words of the living God, but the law is like the school of Hillel."[20] It is not necessary to cite multiple talmudic passages to demonstrate the thesis that Judaism does indeed encourage intellectual diversity and opposition; they are available in abundance.

Our concern will be the characterization of the form of creativity that is the product of independent thought in a context of abiding commitment and unfailing obedience, that is, the delineation of the *Jewish* variety of creativity. A few distinctions, introduced at this juncture, will contribute to its clarification.

First, creativity has two forms. One of these occurs in an ambience of maximum freedom in which there are no self-imposed restraints to interfere with the creative expression of the human personality. It is not surprising that this variety of creativity has received wide sanction and endorsement in American society. Freedom is often regarded as indispensable to creative expression, and it is not difficult, from this assumption, to leap to the conclusion that the larger the freedom, the greater the creativity. On another view, creativity, in its most desirable form, emerges in a climate in which the personality who seeks self-expression experiences himself as bound by obligations and commitments, so that his creative act, which indeed is an act of freedom, is consistent with and an elaboration of the commitments he has undertaken. It is the second of these forms of creativity that is characteristic of the Jewish view.

Second, *creativity* and *progress* are not identical in meaning, though the notion of progress contains creativity as one of its components. The idea of progress presupposes the existence of an identified goal whose realization is sought. The step-by-step movement towards it is a creative process that is simultaneously progressive because it allows mankind or even a single community to advance in the direction of the goal. It is, then, not sufficient that a procedure be novel for it to be called progressive; it must, in addition, lead in the desired direction. On the other hand, the mere novelty of an event, resulting from human conscious effort, entitles it to be identified as creative. In the light of this distinction, it may be concluded that Judaism assigns little value to creativity unless it is a phase of a process leading to genuine progress.

Third, three different kinds of processes may be described as creative: (1) one which utilizes a prevalent method in a new area to realize a received goal; (2) one which introduces a new method to advance to an existing goal; and (3) one which exchanges one goal for another.

The first approach is employed in science. It would be reckless to attempt to change scientific method, which ultimately depends on observation and experimentation, and to substitute for it another which does not rely on empirical evidence—intuition, perhaps, or *a priori* reason—to discover truths about nature. It cannot be done. Neither does any scientist contemplate the transformation of the scientific goal. Science ultimately seeks to explain and to predict events in the universe by means of scientific laws and theories. It would be folly to tamper with the received goals of science. The ever-expanding novelty, creativity, and progress of science is essentially due to its determination to apply classic methods in new areas of research to achieve steady and unchanging goals. It is for this reason that progress in science is visible and dramatic. Achievements are generally cumulative. No one can doubt that scientists know more today than they did one hundred or fifty years ago.

The second approach is utilized in art. The goal is beauty; it is essentially permanent and unchanging. One may argue about the meaning of this concept and even claim that the experience of beauty is not uniform (after all, people do differ with respect to matters of taste), but philosophers of esthetics will generally grant that the purpose of art is to generate objects of beauty. The methods used in art, on the other hand, are constantly changing. Today, there are media for artistic expression which simply did not exist a few centuries ago; photography, for instance. There are also techniques that were not employed in the past, such as the stream-of-consciousness style in literature. While the goal is the same today as in the past, the methods constantly undergo transformation, and thus progress in art is not vertical, as in science, that is to say, it is not cumulative, but horizontal. The realm of art has a wider extension presently than it had before, but it cannot be said that, in some significant sense, mankind has over the centuries, moved closer to the achievement of the ideal.

The third approach is utilized most often in ethics and social theory. The difference between these domains and that of art is striking. The claim is rarely heard that a classic art object, venerated in the past, is no longer to be included in the realm of the beautiful. The claim *is* made that the domain of beauty is expanded by contemporary creations. It is otherwise in the case of morality and social theory. One philosopher, for example, explicitly challenged the legitimacy of moral creeds that enjoyed universal endorsement for wide stretches of human history. He wrote, "We need a *critique* of moral values, *the value of these values* is for the first time to be called into question."[21] A similar situation prevails in social theory. The patterns of capitalism are, as is well known, totally rejected in communist ideology. Hence, while in art, the creative thrust depends on the introduction of new methods, in ethics and social theory, the fashionable view is that creativity depends on the formulation of new goals.

It is obvious, however, that no forward movement is evident when, for example, the ethical goal of man is changed from that of maximizing human potential to the pursuit of pleasure or the quest for power. No significant progress is evident when a society in which freedom is a paramount objective is transformed in such a way that the novel emphasis is no longer liberty but the equal distribution of goods. It is for this reason that it is possible to deny that progress has been made in ethical conduct and social living over the centuries. Many believe that the moral character of human life a hundred years ago was significantly superior to what it is today. One can also argue, and cogently, that life in a totalitarian society today is no less cruel and intolerable than it was millennia ago. The diabolical savagery of the Nazis in World War II Germany was indeed incomparable. The reason for the lack of progress in the moral and social arenas can be traced, in some measure at least, to the circumstance that mankind has lived with the tragic illusion that progress in these domains can be made, not by the disciplined struggle to reach ever closer to human ideals, but by subjecting them to transformations. But such a procedure involves merely a change in direction, not a step forward.

It is evident that the first variety of creativity allows a minimum of freedom but provides the potential for a maximum of progress. The scientist is subject to a rigorous discipline. He is constrained by both method and aim, which it is not his to alter. His task is to apply them to ever novel domains in order to bring new spheres of experience into scientific control so that man may be able to shape his destiny. It is the realm in which progress is most evident.

Judaism is committed to the view that this form of creativity is also indispensable in the domain of ethics and religion. Progress is not to be achieved by frequently transforming religious and moral ideals, but by adopting the discipline of method and goals, and by engaging in intellectual endeavor and debate, to discover ever more effective ways of realizing the aims of Jewish life. Thus, the intellectual individualism of Judaism parallels, in many significant ways, the intellectual individualism of science.

IV

Judaism is ruggedly individualistic. It has not adopted that form of individualism that advocates granting to an individual the right to do as he wishes. It does encourage those forms of individualism that reveal moral courage, that express the value of human life, and that inspire theoretical exploration, the better to understand and the easier to progress.

10

Human Rights

The theme of human rights is perennially the focus of serious and heated dialogue; it will be revealing to explore the Jewish view on the subject. This enterprise is particularly valuable because the struggle for such rights can be traced to ancient Jewish roots. Indeed, it would not be difficult to defend the claim that an understanding of the Jewish doctrine will contribute to the illumination of the concept for its contemporary advocates.

We must address a number of philosophic issues that are generated by the debate on this problem. It is well known that Judaism places greater emphasis on obligations than it does on rights; what are the implications of this emphasis? A satisfactory response to this question must also exhibit the relationship between rights and obligations. But the more important question is: how are we to interpret the basic notion of *human* rights? It is generally believed that such rights differ in some essential way from other forms of right. For one thing, human rights are held to belong to every member of the human race irrespective of agreements. It is also believed that whether one belongs to a democratic, communistic, monarchial, or even a totalitarian community, he has equal claim to the identical set of human rights. Is it possible to justify such beliefs?

117

I

It can be argued, from a purely logical point of view, that wherever there are obligations, there are rights. One philosopher has maintained, as already indicated above, that obligations and rights are correlative. He writes:

> We may assume that "right" and "duty" are correlative terms: A man has a right to perform a certain act A if, and only if, it is not his duty to refrain from performing A; and he has a duty to perform A if, and only if, he does not have the right to refrain from performing A.[1]

Similarly, if obligations are imposed on one person with respect to another, the latter has rights with respect to the former. If a husband has the obligation to support his wife, his wife has the right to be supported. Conversely, if one has rights in relation to another, the latter may have obligations to the former. If a student who paid tuition has the right to receive an education, the university that contracted to supply it has the obligation to do so.

Notwithstanding the correlative character of rights and obligations, there is a considerable difference between deducing obligations from rights and inferring rights from obligations. One major difference is the way in which the notion of freedom is defined in these contrasting perspectives. Those to whom human rights are paramount, and who recognize obligations as legitimate only if they flow from rights, will insist that human freedom is to be construed in terms of the right to do whatever one wishes so long as one does not interfere with others in the pursuit of their inclinations. Indeed, this is the American point of view. If, however, obligations are assigned priority, as is the case in Judaism, acting on inclination receives limited sanction. Freedom, in the Jewish perspective, though it is valued and celebrated, is defined, not in terms of the right to do what we want, but in terms of the power to do what we should, that is, in terms of the capacity to fulfill our obligations.[2] This is one crucial distinction that results from the polarity in emphasis; there are others.

A perspective in which rights are assigned priority is one which fosters self-directedness, a paramount concern with oneself. In such an emphasis, importance is assigned, not to *relations* that attach person to person, but to the person himself, that is, the individual. It is true that, even in such an ambience, people respond to obligations; but they do so because they recognize that the assumption of obligations will serve to secure their rights, and this is their essential thrust. Those, however, for whom obligations are prior are other-directed. They perceive themselves primarily as the bearers of obligations, and even their rights are understood to be functions of the obligations of others to them. They perceive relations between persons as more essential than persons. Hence, while the rights-oriented individual is ego-centered, the obligation-oriented individual is society-centered.

One character that belongs primarily to a nation whose members are society-oriented rather than self-oriented is a sense of solidarity that ties citizens together in community. Community is not at all to be defined in terms of the existence of a variety of institutions, but in terms of relationships that express obligations that one is prepared to assume for others. It is obligations, not rights, that stand at the basis of the unity that characterizes community. Obviously, community also exists in a society that is self-oriented, because obligations are imposed—since they are deduced from rights—even in such a political environment. But the degree of unity is ultimately a function of the depth of the sense of obligation experienced by citizen towards citizen, and that is strongest in an ambience in which emphasis is placed on the values of society-centeredness.

Another, and very important, consequence of assigning priority to obligations is the rejection of the claim, often maintained by those who believe rights to be paramount, that an individual has unlimited rights with respect to his own person. By way of clarification, it should be noted that rights, in the classic sense, are interests on which legitimacy has been conferred. It is not necessary in this context to delineate the source of such legitimacy; at bottom, it depends on the moral or political theory that one adopts. It is important, however, to grasp the point that a course of action which receives moral sanction will not be a right unless it simultaneously serves an interest. Obligations too, it needs to be stressed, according to the theory that assigns priority to rights, are to be defined in terms of interests. The difference between the two is that a man will perceive a course of action as a right if it responds to his interests immediately, and as an obligation if the direct consequence of the action is experienced as depriving him of something he would like to retain (an immediate interest), even while his perception of the remote consequences is that they are favorable to him (a long-term interest). Under these circumstances, he may be prepared to perform the action which he will describe as an obligation.

Now if our system of political values begins with rights and acknowledges only those obligations that they imply, it cannot be maintained that an individual's rights with respect to himself are limited. All his obligations, in such a context, depend on his consent, which he would be inclined to grant—through an instrumentality such as the social contract—only if they serve what he perceives to be his interests. Either an action serves what he sees as his immediate interests, in which case the rule that formulates it expresses a right, or it serves remote, overpowering interests, in which case it is an obligation; in either case, justification is achieved by showing that his interests are served. Our conclusion inevitably is that in a rights-oriented, self-centered society, a human being has no obligations with respect to himself that are not subservient to his interests as he understands them, and that when he perceives an action, on balance, as in his interests, there is no reason for him to refrain from undertaking it; that is, his rights with respect to his own person are unlimited.

It is such a perspective that informs a legal system which allows abortion. Even the right to suicide could not be denied on the basis of such a theory. The argument is that every human being has complete rights over his life and his body. Such a claim is defensible only in a society which is rights-oriented and person-centered.

In an obligation-oriented society, on the other hand, while rights are indeed defined as legitimatized interests, obligations are delineated in a manner which renders considerations of interests irrelevant. This is not to say that the fulfillment of obligations will not, at least on occasion, serve the interest of the agent; it is rather to say that interests never provide the basis for the justification of an obligation.

There are a variety of theories which discover sources of obligation in circumstances other than individual interests. Such, for example, is the theory of natural law. It conceives of the existence of something in nature—it may be the nature of the universe or human nature—that is legislative for all mankind. In the event that the source of obligation is associated with human nature, it may be identified with social imperatives that arise out of the need to assure social peace and progress, or with reason (classical rationalists have argued that the contemplation of the inner contents of the mind will reveal moral principles that impose obligations on all), or with conscience (whose nature is construed as issuing moral commands to all). In any case, interests play no role in the definition of the concept of obligation. Another such theory is theological. It claims that the essential source of human obligation is the will of God.

Obviously, no moral theory which regards obligations as paramount and defines them independently of individual interests will readily accept the notion that a human being has unlimited rights with respect to his own person. Such questions as whether abortion is allowed or suicide permitted will have to be resolved on the basis of considerations other than the fact that such actions serve the interests of the individual confronted with the choice.

II

Having clarified the concept of rights and their relationship to obligations, we turn now to an examination of the notion of *human rights*.

To begin with, they need to be distinguished from contractual rights. The latter are alienable—I can surrender my rights to a variety of things by contract. By entering into a marital, hence contractual, relationship with one person, I give up my right, for the duration of the marriage, to enter into a similar relationship with another person. I can transfer by sale my right to a piece of land of which I am the present owner. It is popularly held that I cannot do this with rights identified as human—for example, in the classical American view, the right to life, liberty, and the pursuit of happiness. The American Declaration of Independence describes these as inalienable, that is, nontransferable. It follows that they are not acquired by means of a social contract. If they were, they could be surrendered, and they would not be inalienable.

Are human rights natural? Presumably, if one may speak of natural laws, that is, natural obligations, it should be equally permissible to speak of natural rights. Modern philosophical literature, however, rejects the view that there are such things as *natural* rights or obligations. The criticism of such notions derives essentially from the observation that an "ought" cannot be deduced from an "is." Nature is described in terms of facts, that is, statements that employ the word *is*; while rights and obligations are formulated in statements that involve the word *ought*. From the fact that smoking *is* not conducive to health, it does not follow logically that one *ought* not to smoke. Such a conclusion calls for an additional premise; for example, I ought not to do that which is detrimental to health. Even if the natural law is construed as prescribing a precept of conduct, for example, an imperative (derived from either reason or the conscience) which prohibits theft, one is presented with merely a fact. When the nature of man is considered, it is discovered, as a matter of fact, that reason or conscience issues commands relative to human conduct. To derive a duty from this fact, there is still needed the additional premise to the effect that I have an obligation to obey such commands. It is not a contradiction to say: I am aware of the fact that reason commands, but I do not believe that I must obey. Natural facts of whatever nature do not logically imply obligations and, by the same token, rights. Human rights, therefore, are not natural either; how then justify the claim that every human being is endowed with such rights and in a manner as to render them inalienable?

There are contemporary attempts to find justification for the claim that to be human is to possess a collection of rights not available to nonhuman species on grounds other than agreements or nature. According to one view, to assert human rights is to formulate the significance conditions of moral discourse. This means, in effect, that any society which understands and accepts moral precepts and judges actions such as theft or homicide as morally repugnant has, in fact, acknowledged that human beings have special rights. One cannot speak of murder as criminal (in a nonjuridical, moral, sense) if he does not believe in the right to life. If one objects to the caste system which prevents an individual from rising above his current economic and social status and pronounces it to be evil, he inevitably believes in the human right of freedom. Another interpretation has it that any society in which, for example, A is a human right is one that requires a justification for any interference with the exercise of A on the part of one of its citizens.[3]

On both these interpretations, however, human rights are not the kinds of things that have legitimacy, but are rather the consequences of existing perceptions among society's members with respect to the kind of conduct that they are willing to accept. That such rights are generally acknowledged within a society is either implicit in human discourse (the first view) or expressed in human attitudes (the second view). In either case, statements of human rights do not formulate *norms* which imply obligations, but *facts* which are essential conditions for the moral precepts to be effective in society. If a society were totally amoral, that is, if moral terms were not at all employed in discourse or no justification were required to interfere with another's actions (the only obstacle to such interference being retaliation by the individual assaulted and by his associates), its citizens could not make a claim to human rights. These interpretations, therefore, represent a radical departure from the classic notion, according to which, such rights are possessed by all irrespective of the political facts that characterize the life of a particular society. It would appear, therefore, that philosophical criticism of the notion of human rights has driven its contemporary defenders to the conclusion that they belong to the category of sociological fact rather than that of ethical norm.

The Jewish view on human rights is that, in the first place, they are deduced from obligations; second, the latter are divinely prescribed; third, the religiously minded individual believes that it is his duty to abide by them and, consequently, to respect the rights that these obligations imply. Further clarification is essential.

To begin with, all human rights derive from God, that is, man is not himself the source of sanction of such rights. I have argued elsewhere that God is the only being with respect to whom a person has any obligations.[4] We often have the occasion to fulfill obligations to God by performing specifically prescribed actions to man; but we never have obligations to man. This holds true of rights as well. Whatever rights we possess have been conferred by God directly (as in the case of the right of Jews to the Holy Land) or flow from obligations imposed by God upon others to behave in prescribed ways to us. All our rights, therefore, have their origin and sanction in God.

Further, not all obligations imposed by God on man imply human rights. If a right can appropriately be regarded as human only when it is applicable to all mankind, it follows that it is only universal obligations that are associated with human rights. Particularistic obligations, addressed to the Jewish community, whose members, by Jewish standards, carry a larger burden of obligations, may imply rights, but these are preferably designated as Jewish rather than human. I have an obligation to admonish a fellow Jew who, for example, violates without compunction the laws of the Sabbath (which only a Jew is required to observe).[5] Accordingly, it is a Jew, and not a gentile, who has a right to be admonished; this is, then, a Jewish, not a human, right.

Human rights are deduced from those obligations which define duties for all mankind; from the Jewish standpoint, these are the seven Noachide commandments. Murder and theft are prohibited; therefore, there are human rights to life and personal property. Adultery is forbidden; it is, therefore, a human right that the institution of marriage shall be respected and not violated.

There is a universal obligation, in every society, to establish courts in order to adjudicate conflicts and to implement the ideal of justice; it is, consequently, a human right to live in a just society.[6]

These rights, deduced from those of the seven obligations which relate to man's behavior to man, are not merely universal; they are also inalienable. I cannot surrender my right to life; the attempt to do so is tantamount to the suspension of the obligations upon others to refrain from taking my life—and this I clearly do not have the right to do. Even the act of suicide represents a violation of the prohibition on murder; I do not have the power to void such an obligation. I cannot authorize another to steal, even from me. I can present him with that which belongs to me as a gift, but I cannot allow him to take something from me by theft. One does not have the right to allow his wife to cohabit with a stranger. Nor does he have the right to allow unjust procedures to be applied by the judicial system in his land. In sum, these rights are both universal and inalienable; they may justifiably be designated as human.

III

There does not appear, however, to be general agreement with respect to the rights that may be identified as "human"; and there need not be. The reason is that it is not necessary to define a human right as one which is universally recognized to be such, but rather as one which, *in any given theory*, is acknowledged to belong inalienably to all mankind. Different ideologies identify diverse sets of rights as belonging to this category. The classic American view emphasizes life, liberty, and the pursuit of happiness; in Judaism, it is life, property, respect for the marital bond, and a just society. No doubt, other communities whose patterns are controlled by alternative commitments may underscore other rights. They will, however, be regarded as human in each perspective if, in that perspective, they are believed to belong, in an inalienable manner, to all.

The problem of finding a set of rights universally acknowledged to be human arises not merely from the circumstance that varying ideologies focus attention on different sets of rights, but that even those rights which are designated as human in every political community are not necessarily understood in the same way. It is generally granted that freedom is a human right. In a democracy, American style, it refers to the right of any human being to act as he wishes as long as he does not interfere with others in their efforts to do the same. In communist ideology, it is interpreted in terms of a certain conformity to the laws of necessity—as in the following passage, "Freedom therefore consists in the control over ourselves and over external nature which is founded on knowledge of natural necessity."[7] Judaism, as we had the occasion to notice above, defines freedom in terms of the power to fulfill obligations. It is not likely that any human right will be portrayed identically in every culture—not even the right to life itself. In some cultural milieus, this right secures the safety of each individual against attack by others. In other cultural environments, it also refers to society's obligation to assure an acceptable quality of life for all its citizens.

It follows that human rights, though they are regarded as universal, do not refer to rights that are culturally unconditioned and acknowledged by all, but to those recognized by a particular culture which holds them to be applicable to all. A society's beliefs concerning human rights are ultimately an expression of its basic attitudes to man and the fundamental values it associates with human life and existence. The element of cultural relativity with respect to the perception of what constitutes a human right is an inevitable consequence. What holds for the science of mechanics is also valid for political science. One cannot describe a motion without first specifying a frame of reference; one cannot identify a human right without taking into account the culture which gives it both its meaning and its emphasis.

Different cultures, because of their very character, hold different rights to be human. The ideology of communism focuses on the right of equality in the enjoyment of material goods. It expresses its conception in the well-known slogan, "From each according to his abilities, to each according to his needs." The emphasis here is on the ability to produce material objects and on the human need for material things essential to life. Given the materialistic orientation of communism, it is not surprising that human rights are identified with that which communism takes to be most important in the life of man and society, namely, the material basis for human existence.

For American democracy, human rights consist of life, liberty, and the pursuit of happiness. Its fundamental motivation is the realization of an ambience in which each citizen may engage in an unimpeded struggle for self-realization. Human rights are deduced from a perception of the arrangements that need to be in place in society to assure the possibility of personal fulfillment. Such arrangements are those which maximize opportunities for life, liberty, and the pursuit of happiness.

As important as it is in a democratic context, and the American Jewish commitment to this ideal notwithstanding, Judaism does not accept the notion that freedom, in its American sense, is a human right. On the Jewish view, we do not have a *right* to do as we wish; we merely have *permission* to do so. In a well-known passage, Maimonides writes, "Permission is given to every man; if he wants to direct himself towards the good way, he may do so; and if he wants to direct himself towards the evil path and to be a scoundrel, he may do so."[8] The Hebrew word used by Maimonides to describe the kind of prerogative granted to the Jew is *reshut*, which means "permission," rather than *zekhut*, which means "right." The term *permission* does not carry with it the kind of legitimacy that we normally associate with that which is designated by the word *right*. The Jew then does not have the right to behave in an evil manner even while he is permitted to do so.

To the Jew, human rights grow out of moral concerns. They flow from obligations imposed on man by divine decree. They are implied by the duties that every human being has to defend the life of another, to avoid encroachment on the property of another, to respect the marriage bond, and to contribute to the establishment of a just society whose institutions will enforce social patterns that will enhance the inclination to respect life, property, and the marital relation. The ultimate basis of human rights is an abiding concern with moral commitment.

IV

Judaism does not perceive human rights as anthropocentric. Nor is it inconsistent with Judaism to argue for cultural relativity in the perception of what constitutes a human right. Its own doctrine is based on moral considerations—its views with respect to the obligations that every man has to his fellow man—and a theological axiom, namely, God is the ultimate source of all human rights.

11

Democracy

The principle of democracy requires that those who exercise sovereignty in any of its forms—executive, legislative, and judicial—shall be elected representatives of the governed. Since it is rare for any individual to enjoy the unanimous support of all citizens, the principle of the majority is introduced to make available a procedure that will assure the possibility of arriving at a decision when there is more than one aspirant to a public office. The latter principle is also employed to conclude a debate when different views are held in legislative and judicial deliberations.

The principle of democracy, therefore, contains two essential components: (1) It holds that decisions taken by those who represent the people in government shall have the consent of those who elected them. (2) It regards the principle of the majority as a desirable and valid means of ending disputes.

Our objective will be to exhibit the extent to which Jewish views on these claims are consistent with the experience of democracy. It cannot be doubted that democratic procedures have obtained in Jewish communities across the ages, but the question remains whether this phenomenon is the result of social and political exigencies or an expression of halakhic precepts.

I

When the right to exercise power derives from a divine source, the approval of those who must submit to it is not essential—neither in the theological nor in the political domain. Moses and the prophets did not have to stand for election, and it was sufficient for ancient monarchs to receive prophetic designation and confirmation by the Sanhedrin.[1] In the postprophetic period, approval by those over whom authority was to be exercised was often perceived to be mandatory for both religious and political leaders. The Talmud declares, as a general principle and without characterizing the nature of the leader in question, "A leader is not appointed over the community without consultation with the community."[2] History records that, in the medieval period and in the case of rabbinic leadership, Rabbenu Tam, Rashbam, Rabban, and one hundred and fifty rabbis issued a decree forbidding a rabbi to assume the role of spiritual head of a community without its endorsement.[3] It would appear that this was equally the case with those who were charged with the administration of the social and economic affairs of a community.

In fact, it was precisely the endorsement of the community that constituted the basis of the authority and/or power exercised by its political leaders. Jewish law, for example, grants to the community's elected representatives extraordinary prerogatives. Rabbi Mosheh Isserles declares, "It is a custom in all communities that the leaders in their own cities are like the Great Sanhedrin, and they may apply lashes and punish and deprive people of their property."[4] How are we to justify the acquisition of such prerogatives by the few over the many?

There are three talmudic concepts that appear relevant to the process of designating community leaders: (1) the idea of agency (shelihut), that is, leaders are viewed as agents of their constituents; (2) the idea of judicial authority (shipput), that is, the community, by an act of election, confers upon its representatives the status of judges; and (3) the notion of sovereignty (malkhut), that is, the leaders receive from the people the status held in ancient days by the people's political rulers. One rabbinic author of responsa, for example, in the course of a discussion of a talmudic issue, declared, "The leaders of the community are apparently merely the community's agents. . . . And [citing another opinion with which he ostensibly does not agree] even if you will say that the community leaders are like a court, a view that was espoused by Rabbi Israel Isserlein (in his volume entitled *Terumat ha-Deshen*), etc."[5] Others, however, deduce the status of leaders from the concept of the sovereign. Rabbi Abraham Isaac Kook, in a discussion of the halakhic basis for the political authority exercised by the present-day leaders of the Jewish state, declares, "It is certainly the case that the leaders approved by the people, designated to administer the affairs of the people . . . clearly occupy the status of a king."[6] It may not be necessary to limit this principle to those who are the national leaders of a Jewish state; it may be applicable to all who are elected to administer the affairs of their respective communities.

It could be argued, and I believe cogently, that the three talmudic concepts from which the status of leaders is derived can be reduced to two. The passage cited above in the name of Rabbi Isserles, which speaks of the prerogatives of leaders to sentence a transgressor to lashes and to deprive him of his property, is a comment on a passage in the Code of Jewish Law (the *Ḥoshen Mishpat*) whose author (Rabbi Joseph Karo) speaks of the right of duly designated leaders to render decisions which are contrary to the law (in circumstances in which the law, for its own procedural reasons, cannot be applied) in order to set limits to antisocial behavior. But such a right is characteristic of a sovereign rather than a juridical entity because the latter by its very nature is obliged to apply the letter of the law. The political leader, for the sake of improving social conditions (*tikkun ha-olam*), is allowed, on occasion, to evade the law. When a similar right is granted to a court, it is because it too is, at times, endowed with a political, rather than a merely judicial, prerogative. This transformation in the character and function of the court was often necessitated by the circumstance that political leadership among the Jewish people was either nonexistent or functioned ineffectively. Hence, the statement that the leaders of a community are like the Great Sanhedrin, which was entitled to punish and to deprive people of their property contrary to the prescriptions of the law, is intended to assert that the actions of leaders are in the same category as those of the Great Sanhedrin when it functioned in a sovereign, that is, a political rather than juridical, capacity. Accordingly, the leaders of the community may be regarded from two, rather than three, possible talmudic perspectives: they are either the agents of the people or they exercise some element of sovereign power conferred by the people.

What are the implications that flow from these two ways of interpreting the status of political leadership? First, it is necessary to direct attention to something they have in common. Even if agency is the basis for the authority exercised by elected leaders, it must be assumed that the community, as such, is endowed with extraordinary prerogatives not possessed by individuals. For if the result of agency is that the leaders are empowered to act contrary to law, that is, as sovereigns would, then certain powers must be vested in the people (which they can assign to leaders through agency) which individuals do not possess. Hence, in both perspectives, the community is perceived as endowed with extraordinary powers. Indeed, it may be regarded as the equivalent, in political power, of both prophet and Sanhedrin, who together, in ancient days, were vested with the prerogative of designating political leaders.

Nevertheless, there is a crucial difference between the view that a ruler is an agent and that which assigns him to the category of a sovereign. The thrust of the principle of agency, which declares that "a man's agent is like himself,"[7] is that the actions of the agent are to be attributed to the individual who designated him in the first place. If A authorizes B, as his agent, to fulfill an obligation, then this principle allows us to regard the action of B as if it were performed by A. The principle that confers sovereign power does not require such attribution. Further, according to the principle of agency as normally construed, it is the obligation of the agent to act in conformity to the will of the principal who designated him. According to the principle of sovereignty, one who is designated the political leader has the right to legislate for the community irrespective of what its will might be.

It follows that just as in the case of individual agency, an agent has no authority beyond the limits explicitly specified by the one he represents, so in the case of the community, the authority of the leader, if he is perceived in terms of agency, is limited by the bounds placed upon him by his electors. It might even be urged that the leader may represent those who voted for him but that his decisions have no validity with respect to those who opposed him. Such a view is expressed by one rabbinic sage, who declared that the majority does not have the right to compel the minority to accept any judgment of which the latter does not approve.[8] Hence, if the majority authorized a leader to act in its behalf and the minority did not participate in the election, it is not subject to the will of that leader.

It is a classic question often debated in democratic forums. Is the elected representative obligated to try to discern the will of the people and act in conformity to his perception of what that will might be, or is it his duty to use his own best judgment in behalf of the people? If leadership is interpreted in terms of agency, it would follow that the leader must be responsive to the inclinations of those whom he represents; if it is construed in terms of sovereignty, however, the leader's use of his own judgment would appear to be in order.

There is another way of putting this distinction. The question may be asked: does the act of election confer power or authority? If the status of leadership derives from the principle of agency, it can be cogently argued that the leader possesses only *authority* to act in consonance with the will of the people who are the source of his authority. The view that election confers power presupposes no obligation to be responsive to anyone who might have conferred that power. On the latter view, the leaders duly endorsed by the populace acquire the prerogative of administering the affairs of the community in conformity with their own best judgment. Thus, the notion of power can be interpreted in terms of a degree of independence possessed by the one who wields it that is entirely alien to the notion of authority.

It is conceivable that there may be categories of persons in the Jewish community to whom traditional Judaism denies the right to wield power without depriving them of the prerogative to serve as leaders in the capacity of agents. It is possible that, contrary to the view of Maimonides, women fall into this category. Maimonides states quite explicitly that women may not be assigned *serarah*, that is, any position in which they would be exercising power. In a passage in which he discusses the types of personalities who may not serve in a sovereign capacity within the Jewish community, he refers to both an individual born of a non-Jewish mother and a woman and writes:

> A convert is not designated a king even after many generations unless his mother is of the Jewish community, for it is written, "You may not designate over yourself a stranger who is not your brother"; and this applies not only to kingship but to all exercise of power—he cannot be a general or a commander of a hundred or of ten; nor even in charge of a water canal from which he distributes to the fields. It is certainly the case that a judge or a president [of the Sanhedrin] shall be selected from the Jewish community. We do not designate a woman as a sovereign, for it is written, "[Place] over yourself a king," but not a queen. Similarly, only men are designated to all positions of command within the Jewish community.[9]

The ancient Jewish king clearly exercised power, rather than merely authority, over the people. The rabbis interpreted the phrase which mandated the designation of a sovereign as intended to elevate someone to inspire fear and reverence among the community's members.[10] Apparently, Maimonides regarded all exercise of social and political authority as ultimately an exercise of power and traced all rights to the use of such power to the principle of sovereignty. Leaders were not merely agents; they were endowed with some aspect of sovereign power. If, however, the status of the leader is not in the same category as that of a sovereign, that is, he exercises authority rather than power, it is conceivable that, while women may not serve as kings or rule as queens, they may, as agents of the community, assume authority. It is clear that, from a talmudic standpoint, the principle of agency applied to women as well. The Code of Jewish Law states quite explicitly, "An individual may designate as an agent a man or a woman. . . . Since they have intelligence and are among those who are obligated to perform commandments, they may serve as agents in business matters."[11] In addition, the agent may be authorized to act according to his understanding of what is desirable, and if the one who designates him specifies that he is willing to accept any conclusion at which the agent arrives, the acts of the agent are final for the principal. As Maimonides writes:

> If the principal declared to the agent that he will accept the decisions of the agent whether they are advantageous or disadvantageous to him; then even if the agent sold something worth one hundred for a dinar or bought something worth a dinar for a hundred, the principal cannot change his mind.[12]

It follows that if a woman may serve as an agent, she may also be assigned the authority to make decisions according to her perception of what may be desirable in a situation in which she is authorized to act; and if the understanding is that, in virtue of her election, all her decisions are to be accepted by those who assigned agency, she may act in accordance with her personal assessments. Such could be the arrangement when a woman is elected to a position of leadership. Her status can be perceived as that of the community's agent who has been authorized to make decisions all of which, by initial consent, will be accepted by the community that elected her.

In a similar vein, some rabbis distinguish between the prerogatives of a leader in the Jewish community and those of persons who are designated to act, for example, on behalf of a professional or trade group. The question had already been raised before: can the majority and the leaders that they designate impose their decisions on a minority which rejects the decisions or repudiates the leaders? Some rabbinic interpreters argue that while a minority is obliged to accept the judgments of communal leaders, it is not compelled to abide by the decrees of organizational representatives.[13] The reason may be that, while the communal leader occupies the status of a sovereign, the group representative is merely an agent, and thus his authority is not relevant to those who failed to endorse his leadership.

It is this distinction between power and authority that also illuminates the ancient prophetic response to the demand of the people that a king be designated to rule them. When the prophet Samuel confronted such a call, he reacted with hesitation and distress. Notwithstanding biblical sanction, he resisted complying with the people's demand. The reason was that, in his perception, while authority might be assigned to humans, power belonged primarily and essentially to God; and though the Bible authorized the appointment of a monarch, the prophet interpreted such sanction as a response to social necessity rather than as an ideal arrangement.

The prophet, the rabbi, and the judge, on the other hand, are to be distinguished from the monarch in that they are granted only authority. Their primary aim is to interpret God's will to man, to apply divine precepts to human conduct. They are fundamentally *shelukha de-rahmunah*, the messengers of God assigned the task of molding a community in consonance with the divine will. It is otherwise with a sovereign who, on his own understanding and with his own resources, responds to a situation which demands some form of action, in accordance with principles that he formulates for himself. This is the essence of human power—the use of available means to reach human goals by rules that man devises for himself—and the prophet perceives its use as an encroachment on the prerogatives of the Almighty. Judaism fully understands human authority, but notwithstanding the fact that it is recognized as indispensable, Judaism is suspicious of human power.

II

The second essential component in the idea of democracy is that of rule by majority. This rule is, in truth, a form of a larger majority principle, namely, that of *rov*. The latter is involved in the determination of facts, the application of law to facts, and the enactment of laws. The Talmud offers the following examples. If a community has nine meat stores, eight kosher and one non-kosher, and a cut of meat is found on a street, the assumption is made that it comes from one of the majority stores, and the meat is judged to be kosher. This is a determination of a fact made on the basis of the majority principle. If a court is considering the guilt or innocence of a defendant with respect to a crime that, for example, calls for a death penalty, if most members of the court decide in favor of the defendant, he is declared innocent. Here the principle of the majority involves the application of law to fact; for both must be determined before sentence is pronounced. The latter procedure is also required by the biblical imperative *aharei rabbim le-hatot*, follow majority *opinion*, a special case of *rov*, the more general majority principle. There is another application of the narrower principle which involves the determination of law. If a question could not be answered by the lower courts, eventually it had to reach the Great Sanhedrin. If its members knew the answer, they would give it; if they were not clear as to how to resolve the matter, Maimonides writes, reflecting a passage in the Talmud, "They would debate the issue until there was universal agreement, or they would take a vote and follow the majority."[14]

A question may be asked about the domain of application of the narrower principle. Is the legitimacy that it confers on the majority view applicable only to rabbinic disputes, or is it equally relevant to debates among communal leaders? The following rabbinic commentary addresses itself to this question:

With respect to your question whether two or three people in the city may exclude themselves from an agreement arrived at by the community or from the edict it issued with respect to any matter, know that with regard to a question affecting the community, the Torah said, "Follow the majority"; hence, on any issue on which the community agrees, we follow the majority; and individuals are obligated to obey all that the community agreed upon. Were this not the case, the community would never conclude any matter. . . . Hence, the Torah declared in all matters that involve communal agreement, "Follow the majority."[15]

It appears, therefore, on this interpretation, that the majority principle applies, not only to the courts, but to leadership in the community as well. The reason that the latter is included in the meaning of biblical verse is that, as a matter of practical necessity, such authority had to be granted to facilitate the administration of community affairs; hence, it had to be contained in the biblical precept.

However, the principle which requires that we follow the majority opinion is not merely a heuristic device introduced to avoid community paralysis in the event leaders are unable to agree. Its application also confers a certain kind of legitimacy on many actions taken by its use that appears to transcend its practical status as an indispensable procedural rule.

This is certainly the case when it is applied in rabbinic disagreements. An interesting and well-known talmudic example is an incident involving a dispute between Rabbi Eliezer and the rabbis with regard to the status of a certain variety of oven. The issue debated is not, at the moment, crucial to this discussion. What is of interest is that, in view of the fact that the rabbis who disputed the view of Rabbi Eliezer constituted a majority, it was their opinion that was taken as authoritative. The Talmud relates that a divine voice was heard declaring that Rabbi Eliezer was correct. Rabbi Joshua responded:

It is not up to heaven. What is the meaning of "It is not up to heaven"? Rabbi Jeremiah declared: The Torah was already given at Mount Sinai; we do not listen to heavenly voices because it is already written in the Torah, "Follow the majority."[16]

Hence, the principle of aharei rabbim le-hatot, that is, follow the majority opinion, appears to carry considerable weight. Rabbis are required to proceed in consonance with the majority opinion, even

if a transcendental source testifies that the conclusion arrived at
by its means is mistaken.

This point receives emphasis in still another rabbinic commentary.

> When the participants in the debate are equal in wisdom or
> approximately so, the Torah informs us that the majority
> opinion will always agree upon the truth, more than the mi-
> nority. And whether they arrived at the truth or not in the
> perception of the one who hears it, the law prescribes that we
> not deviate from the majority.[17]

Nevertheless, the authority assigned to a rabbinic decision on the
basis of the application of the majority rule is not unlimited. It is
unqualified only within certain parameters.

On a question of law, the Talmud is clear. If the law is part
of the written Torah and its prescription can easily be determined
by all, a ruling by even a majority of the Great Sanhedrin that it
is not in force should be ignored. The Talmud considers the
question of an erroneous decision by the Great Sanhedrin which
was accepted and followed by members of the Jewish community.
Under such conditions, whose is the guilt and who must atone?
By way of reply, the following distinction is made. The court is
guilty if it erred in a matter "in which the Sadducees do not agree"
(with the Pharisees; such disagreements focused on the oral law);
while the individuals who acted on the judicial decision are guilty
if the error was in a matter "in which the Sadducees agree" (the
written law).[18] The Sanhedrin's conclusions with respect to the
unrecorded oral tradition do carry with them authority and finality, and its views must be adopted.

The reason that a mistaken decision by the Sanhedrin with
respect to a matter addressed in the written law should be ignored
is that an individual ought to know better. If the correct view is
available in written form, ignorance is no excuse and the greatest
judicial body in the land has no authority to controvert it. It would
not be farfetched to infer that the same argument is relevant to
the determination of facts. A judicial body cannot decide that day

is night or that a horse is a fish. If they did, even by the use of the majority principle, the conclusion would not be valid.

A talmudic example that appears to involve a question of the determination of a fact concerns a dispute between Rabbi Gamaliel who, together with the court over which he presided, accepted the testimony of two witnesses that they had observed the new moon and that *Rosh Ḥodesh*, the first day of the new month, could be consecrated, and Rabbi Joshua, who maintained that as a matter of *fact*, the new moon could not have been observed. It is clear that whether the initial phase of the moon appeared or not is a question of fact, not one of either law or definition. It is a matter that can normally be resolved by observation, that is, by empirical procedures. Notwithstanding, when Rabbi Joshua consulted with Rabbi Akiva, the latter declared that it was ultimately a matter of law—for the act of consecrating the new month does not depend on the fact of the moon's appearance, but on the decision of the court to which the Torah explicitly gave the power to make this determination. The Torah does require, when weighing testimony with respect to the appearance of a new moon, a consideration of the facts and urges the members of the court to take them into account, but it confers validity on the decision taken by the majority irrespective of the facts. Rabbi Joshua also consulted on this issue with Rabbi Dosa, who expanded on the concept of the court's authority but did not maintain that it encompassed rendering decisions contrary to facts. What he did claim, according to subsequent clarification of his views, is that a court possesses authority notwithstanding the circumstance that its members may not be outstanding scholars and jurists.[19]

It would appear that the majority principle carries maximum weight in the instance of legal definition, that is, defining a concept by law. In the case referred to above, involving the status of an oven, with respect to which Rabbi Eliezer and the rabbis disagreed, the question was indeed one of definition. Is an oven structured in the manner described in the relevant passage to be regarded as attached to the ground or not? There are no experimental procedures that could be utilized to answer that question; it requires a definition. In this instance the majority principle could

141

be employed to arrive at a conclusion that is to be regarded as final and that even a heavenly voice cannot countermand.

There is another well-known passage in rabbinic literature which appears to affirm the unqualified validity of decisions arrived at by the Great Sanhedrin. On a biblical verse which instructs a Jew not to deviate from the decisions of the judges "to the right or to the left," Rashi comments, reflecting an interpretation of the *Sifrei*, "Even if you are told that right is left or left is right."[20] It might appear that such a decision may constitute an error in fact; in truth it is ultimately an error in definition. Whether an object is to the right or the left depends on the frame of reference one adopts, and obviously, if A is facing B, what is to the right of A is to the left of B. The determination of a frame of reference is ultimately a matter of definition. Accordingly, it should be fair to conclude that in matters of legal definition, the rabbinic view arrived at by the use of the principle of the majority has finality.

In sum, the Great Sanhedrin was assigned unqualified authority, by majority vote, to decide questions affecting the oral law and matters of legal definition. It did not have the power to suspend a law in the written Torah or to deny a fact ascertainable by all.

III

It is clear that the fundamental principles of democracy, namely, representative government and rule by majority, inhere in Jewish tradition. Though their application is more restricted in a Torah community than in a democratic society, their employment in Jewish life reflects principles that are essentially halakhic in nature.

12

Peace

The question is: what status is peace to be assigned on the scale of political values? Specifically, is peace to be subordinated to the requirements of justice, or shall justice be surrendered in the interests of peace? Which of the two is the more ultimate value? This question presupposes two others, equally crucial. What is the relation between justice and peace? Will peace be achieved with the application of principles of justice, or, perhaps, is the insistence on justice, at least at times, an impediment to peace? Assuming that justice does not necessarily lead to peace, what are the consequences of assigning preference to one over the other? Our concern will be with the Jewish response to these questions.

I

Must peace be achieved in human relations and in society if the demands of justice are met? It is important to note, to begin with, that there are two varieties of peace. One of these is associated with the messianic ideal; it is a peace of a permanent and lasting kind. It involves social relations among groups and individuals which are devoid of tension; it exists in an ambience that leaves no need for a person or group to take measures of protection against another. In prophetic literature, this kind of peace is invariably associated with the universal reign of justice. One example of this is the passage in *Isaiah* which describes the messianic personality as one who, by implementing the requirements of justice, will bring uninterrupted tranquillity to mankind.[1] This kind of peace is the result of transcendental rather than political action; it is, therefore, not relevant to our question. The other variety of peace is one which is temporary, permits tension, and is consistent with the nonviolent struggle for supremacy; it is a condition that is not incompatible with a state of cold war. It is a peace that emerges out of a political context and is, accordingly, the variety with respect to which our question is put.

Now, it should be noted that justice is also of two kinds and that the answer to our question will, at least in measure, depend on the variety that is being considered. Its two forms are implicit in the following talmudic discussion. On the verse in *Zechariah* which declares, "Truth and the judgment of peace shall you execute in your gates,"[2] the rabbis comment, "Where there is judgment there is no peace, and where there is peace there is no judgment. In what circumstances, then, do we find judgment combined with peace? In compromise."[3] It would appear that the forms of justice are: (1) the strict application of a principle which expresses justice as an objective imperative in virtue of certain relevant features of a situation, and (2) a determination of that which might be satisfactory to both litigants in a case and an agreement reflecting their subjective consent to such arrangements. The latter is identified as compromise. This passage of the Talmud asserts, in addition, that one type of justice, namely, the one derived from mutual consent, is, indeed, essential to peace, while the variety that requires the rigorous application of an objective principle is inconsistent with it.

The reason that the strict use of the objective principle is held to be incompatible with peace is twofold. First, the litigants engaged in a confrontation do not necessarily accept the decision of a jurist as a correct implementation of the principle. It is essential, not merely that justice be done, but that it shall be *perceived* by the combatants that it was done. It is often the case that defeated litigants depart from the courtroom with intensified hostility, not merely for their antagonists, but for the court as well. They regard themselves as the victims of gross injustice, and in many instances, are really unable to grasp how justice could require the suffering they will inevitably experience as a result of the decision rendered. Secondly, even if they were to perceive the decision as embodying the principle of justice, their resentments could very well be hardened, if not intensified, by the unpalatable experience of defeat. The ego, even if it recognizes itself in the wrong, suffers anguish when beaten and, in that mood, is not inclined to surrender the satisfactions of hatred.

It is otherwise with compromise, which is based on the consideration that if, for example, A has a financial obligation to B, and B forgives A a portion of it, justice does not demand that A compensate B for the part that he willingly surrendered. This, in effect, is the essence of business agreements. Justice declares that obligations voluntarily assumed and rights voluntarily surrendered, by contract, for example, are binding and enforceable in a court of law. This, also, is the essence of compromise, which involves the voluntary surrender of rights in the interests of resolving a dispute. The advantage of compromise is that while neither perceives justice to have been implemented in an objective sense, both recognize that, in view of their subjective consent, the demands of justice have indeed been met. In addition, both are spared the sense of defeat, and conceivably each may even experience a sense of partial satisfaction. Such an outcome has the potential to restore a relationship of peace.

It has been claimed that compromise is an essential prerequisite to peace, not merely in interpersonal but in international relations. Nations in the grip of war can bring it to an end either by defeating their opponents or by compromising with them. It is argued that the surrender of a nation has the effect of scarring its national ego and prompting it to seek the occasion to wreak revenge. It will not be content to remain at peace so long as its pride lies shattered. In compromise, on the other hand, there is neither victor nor defeated and, consequently, a greater probability of a lasting peace. This, in fact, was the rationale that prompted an American statesman to prevent Israel from achieving a clear-cut victory in the Yom Kippur War.

PEACE 145

The two types of justice can be described in still another way. When the principle of justice is carefully applied independently of the inclinations of the antagonists, the outcome may be said to be a true expression of the ideal; when the results are determined by concession, by the surrender of rights on the part of the litigants, justice is attained but truth is, to some extent, relinquished. An individual may forgo that which is truly his in the interest of securing tranquillity. Indeed, it is the demand that truth inform and invariably guide human relations that has all too frequently been a source of tension and hostility in human life. It appears, therefore, that the pursuit of justice, unaccompanied by the demand that truth be rigorously applied, is a more effective means of achieving peace than is the insistence that justice shall, without exception, be based on truth.

It is, perhaps, for this reason that the implementation of justice in the form of compromise, that is, without simultaneously insisting on the careful exemplification of truth, has been assigned priority over its other form in the *Code of Jewish Law*. The following statement is explicit on this score:

It is an obligation to say to the litigants: Do you want judgment or compromise? If they want compromise, we [the judges] effect a compromise between them. Just as [the judge] is warned not to distort the judgment, so is he warned not to bend the compromise in favor of one rather than the other. And every court which effects compromises constantly is to be praised.[4]

It should, however, be noted that, while this is indeed the principle that has guided Jewish life in the course of its history, not all views expressed in the Talmud coincide with it. There is, for example, the declaration:

The world rests on three things: on justice, on truth, and on peace; Rabbi Muna said: And the three are one—if justice is done, if truth is achieved, peace is accomplished; and all three are included in a single verse, "Truth and the judgment of peace shall you execute in your gates?"; wherever there is judgment, there is peace.[5]

Obviously, the meaning of the verse in *Zechariah* is the subject of a rabbinic dispute. On the interpretation given to it in the passage just cited, justice and peace are intimately interconnected, that is, justice invariably leads to peace, and the question as to which is to be assigned priority cannot arise. In fact, however, this is not the view that has prevailed in Jewish life. To the contrary, justice in the form of compromise is held to contribute to peace; the application of the principle objectively is seen as not always compatible with a peaceful outcome. The question as to which has priority is, then, crucial.

II

It is important to consider the fact that historic as well as halakhic considerations contributed to the determination of the priorities in Jewish life. The historic factor is crucial because the Jewish community, living so often in an alien environment, was frequently threatened to a point where its welfare and its very life were at stake. It is well known that, in times of crisis and turmoil, the Jewish people became the favorite scapegoat of every frustrated group in society, and when anarchy reigned, it was this people that invariably suffered. For reasons of self-preservation, the Jewish interest in peace frequently outweighed other considerations. Nor was this attitude incompatible with rabbinic teaching. The rabbis found biblical justification for the violation of Torah precepts, with some exceptions, whenever even the life of an individual was threatened. This was certainly the case when an entire community faced disaster. Accordingly, the Halakhah also requires that Jews assess their circumstances from a historic perspective. Hence, whatever the halakhic view may be on the question of priority in normal circumstances, the goal of community survival often required that Jews subordinate other considerations to the desperate need to preserve peace.

In normal conditions, however, when the life of a Jew or a community is not threatened, justice, on the Jewish view, takes precedence. This is implicit in all talmudic commentaries which prescribe resistance to government when its enactments are seen to be unfair. One is not obligated to abide by government decrees, opposition to which would not represent a threat to the Jewish community, if these have the effect of obstructing the Jew in the performance of his specifically religious, noneconomic, obligations; or even if they are economic in character, but do not find universal application in the society for which they are enacted—notwithstanding the fact that the failure to obey will generate tensions or even hostilities. In the normal case, therefore, considerations of justice do take priority over social tranquillity. The question that remains, then, is: what are the consequences of reversing this priority?

III

The first result of subordinating justice to the pursuit of peace is that a society in which this perception of values prevails will, in all likelihood, tend to be totalitarian.

This is a conclusion to which we are led by a study of classic political literature. One of the remarkable inferences that students of government are entitled to draw from such a study is that the identical concept which serves as the basis for democracy can also be used as the starting point for the development of a totalitarian doctrine. The concept is that of the social contract. Hobbes used it to justify a system of absolute monarchy; in the philosophies of Locke and Rousseau, it became the rationale for a theory of democracy. This divergence in the results of the application of the identical notion was a consequence of the fact that, while Hobbes regarded peace as the paramount social objective, his philosophical adversaries assigned that role to justice. If the pursuit of peace is "the first law of nature,"[6] justice, in the form of enforcing the claims of citizens against a monarch, may be surrendered. If, on the other hand, justice is assigned the highest rank, citizens must

be granted the power to rearrange the government if they perceive themselves to be the victims of injustice; hence, democracy.

(Alternatively, the concept of the social contract may be viewed
as one which is intended to supply a basis for the definition of
the notion of justice. It presupposes, of course, that justice is not
an abstract concept; that is, the principles of justice are not imposed from some transcendental realm upon mankind, but rather
are the formulae to which, for one reason or another, the members
of society have given their consent. The principles to which citizens
would agree will ultimately depend on their conception of the
kind of social relations that must prevail if they are to achieve a
satisfactory life. If peace is their paramount objective, they will be
prepared, as Hobbes argued, to surrender almost all their rights
to secure peace; in which case justice would consist essentially of
the obligation to obey all edicts proclaimed by the sovereign who
possesses the power to guarantee peace. If peace is assigned a
secondary role, the principles arising out of the social contract,
which together constitute justice, will embody values upon which
citizens confer greater importance—such as freedom, equality,
representative government. These cannot be defended unless action is sometimes taken against government, that is, unless people
are prepared to forgo the blessings of peace.)

It was this type of philosophy that was utilized by political
thinkers in days past to justify revolution, an enterprise that could
not have been undertaken if peace were, indeed, given the highest
rank. It is the same perspective that conferred legitimacy, in contemporary American history, in the era of the civil rights movement, on acts of civil disobedience. It appears that a definition of
justice in a manner that turns it into a function of human social
well-being rather than of peace, together with the perception of
peace as of secondary value, results in a political environment
which is not conducive to totalitarian government.

Jews have always been very much at home in a democratic
society precisely because, in it, justice is viewed as occupying a
superior status. Of course, the principles of justice do not have
the same basis in the Jewish view and in the American perspective.
Judaism recognizes a Transcendental Being as the source of sanc-

tion of these principles, rather than the human condition which expresses itself, by means of the social contract, in enactments to which citizens are prepared to give their assent. Notwithstanding, on this crucial issue, Jewish and American views coincide. Both assign greater importance to the ideal of justice than to that of peace. This circumstance instills in the Jew and the American identical inclinations, that is, to resist, with energy and dedication, any serious trespass by the government on the just rights of citizens. This is, in the Jewish perspective, the core of the ideal of freedom. And even while Jews accommodated themselves to totalitarian governments in order to assure their survival as individuals and as communities during the lengthy period of the diaspora, they found the climate of democracy much more in accord with their most fundamental inclinations.

IV

Another consequence of subordinating justice to peace is the encouragement, in the society in which such priorities exist, of the acceptance of conditions that would normally be regarded as unjust. The irenic individual, that is, the one who is totally committed to peace, will do nothing that can bring turmoil with resulting violence to society, even if he should feel oppressed. It is a view that approaches, though is not identical to, pacifism. Pacifism is the doctrine that rejects violence as a means of resisting an aggressor or of rectifying social conditions which are perceived to be unjust under any conditions. If the pacific posture derives from the view that peace is the supreme political value, there are circumstances in which violence could be justified; for example, when an assault by another eliminates the possibility of peace altogether. There is the old adage which declares that it takes two to make peace, only one to make war. Under such conditions, the irenic approach is not incompatible with the use of violence. Notwithstanding, assigning a higher status to peace, even at the expense of justice, implies the acceptance of every condition no matter how unjust, so long as a challenge to it would disturb the peaceful tenor of human life.

Granted, Judaism, with some exception, also eschews violence as a means of resolving social tensions that reflect conditions of injustice, especially when other approaches are available for the achievement of the same objective. For example, it is likely that Judaism does not endorse revolution as a method of transforming the structure of society, both for reasons of principle and because of pragmatic considerations. Practically speaking, it is not possible to predict the outcome of political turbulence introduced by violence; the results, as history has demonstrated abundantly, may be entirely contrary to the intention that inspired the violence in the first place. But even as a matter of principle, it is preferable to accomplish a social objective without violence, if it is only possible to do so, even if the process is a lengthier one.[7] Indeed, there is such a thing as a hesitation to use violence, not to preserve peace, but because of moral commitments. The latter is the Jewish view.

What then is the difference between the two bases for resisting violence? It appears to lie largely in the extent to which injustice is perceived to exist in society. If peace is the ultimate political goal, there will be a tendency to view conditions that otherwise might be regarded as unfair as morally acceptable; they will be justified on the grounds that they allow peace to be preserved. If, on the other hand, a hesitation to employ methods of violence derives from a commitment to moral principle, that is, a determination to avoid injuring an innocent party, then even while citizens recoil from violence, their sensitivity to injustice in society will not be diminished. The Jewish people exemplifies this combination—a hesitation at the use of violence together with a sensitivity to injustice—dramatically.

The Jewish response to injustice is, therefore, twofold. On the one hand, because of moral sensitivity, Jews tend to resist injustice, in any degree to which it may be exemplified, by all methods that are pacific in character. On the other, Jews will refrain from violence, for reasons of moral commitment, if resorting to it is inconsistent with moral obligation. The peaceful strain in the Jewish character is, therefore, not due to a blind devotion to peace at any price, but to essentially moral considerations.

It may be granted that, notwithstanding the fact that it is justice

which should be assigned the highest status in the Jewish scheme
of political values, rabbinic literature does exhibit a preoccupation,
even a fascination, with peace. There are numerous talmudic passages which emphasize repeatedly that peace is great.[8] The thirst
for peace may be due to the pain and anguish experienced by the
Jew as a result of the devastation visited upon him in the course
of even his early history. It may also be due to the prophetic vision
that associates lasting peace with the messianic era, a condition to
which the Jew always aspires and of which he dreams. It is not,
however, a result of the perception that peace carries with it the
highest political value.

V

The rabbis often extol the virtues of peace; they, nevertheless,
regard justice as of even greater value. This accounts for the high
degree of Jewish moral sensitivity and the willingness of the Jew,
especially in a democratic society, to take action in behalf of those
who are oppressed.

13

Galut

The concept of *galut*, exile, is primarily theological in nature. Religious Jews are familiar with some aspects of its theological meaning. They recite, during the festivals of the Jewish calendar, a prayer which declares that "because of our sins were we *exiled* from our land." Of course, theologically speaking, *galut* means, in addition, alienation, distance from the divine being, and human imperfection.

Galut, however, has political significance as well, and it is on the political ramifications of the theological state identified as *galut* that we shall focus. When a people believes itself to be in *galut*, that consciousness does something to its national character. It colors its relations with the peoples among whom it lives, it introduces an added dimension of unity among the people whose minds and hearts it suffuses, and it inevitably inspires this people to undertake a program—which may indeed be political in nature—to achieve redemption.

I

The sense of *galut* is, in the first place, an awareness of the possession of distinguishing characteristics and of their importance. It is incompatible with any national political and social process in the diaspora whose thrust is homogeneity and uniformity. It prevents anyone possessing this sense from melting into the cultural landscape in which he may happen to find himself. It is a vector pushing in a direction opposite to that of assimilation. It is a powerful force in behalf of the preservation of Jewish identity and commitment.

It is so powerful in its thrust that it was deemed essential to circumscribe the boundaries of its application. One objective of the principle enunciated by the talmudic sage Samuel that "the law of the land is the law"[1] is to prevent the possibility that Jews, affected by a feeling of social alienation due to their sense of exile, would find themselves incapable of involvement even in the world of business affairs. Still another talmudic sage urged his coreligionists to pray for the peace of the kingdom[2] in order that, even while they remained estranged, they could participate in the life of the society in which they lived.

This softening of the sense of distinctiveness notwithstanding, the awareness that he is different, even unique, introduced tension into the Jew's relations with those by whom he was surrounded. On juridical questions, where economic issues were concerned, and in certain political activities, he could, according to rabbinic parameters, appropriate patterns that he found in the country he adopted. In other matters, however, he guided himself by traditions conveyed to him by his Jewish heritage, and his conduct was alien to the social norms that surrounded him. Hence, though he was obligated "to pray for the peace of the kingdom," the isolation that inevitably followed upon his insistence on remaining distinct brought him an abundance of political problems as well. With the exception of the modern era and when he lived in a democratic context, citizenship was not granted to him. He very often remained in his own community, frequently a ghetto, in which life was organized by his own people. It was a government within a government, an aspect of ghetto life that was, in a significant sense, a matter of his own choosing. Even in a democracy his integration into the life of society was less than total.

We can formulate the political consequences of the *galut* mentality with greater precision. In the first place, the political ideal of the *galut*-minded Jew had to diverge from that of his non-

Jewish neighbor. He could never accept the conception of the political goal prevalent in the society in which he found himself as his own ultimate objective. If he lived in a democratic nation and it defined its ultimate purpose in terms of freedom for all its members, he could identify with his countrymen in their assessment of the value of freedom and thank God for its blessings, but in the depths of his being, he would yearn for the opportunity to realize his dream of a return to the land of his ancestors. His ideal was separated by a chasm from those of his neighbors. This was the case even when he recognized the fact that the actualization of his political vision was beyond his capacity and, in the highest degree, improbable in the light of existing conditions. The unlikelihood of achieving his aim did not mitigate his sense of difference.

We must be careful not to draw the implication that the Jew, therefore, was not a completely loyal and patriotic citizen of his adopted country. In fact, the opposite is the case. If the measure of wholehearted patriotism is the extent of sacrifice that a citizen is prepared to make for his country, it may be concluded that, at least among those nations in which the Jew was allowed to enjoy the benefits of citizenship, his loyalty was exemplary. The conduct of the Jew in the United States illustrates this conclusion dramatically. It can be cogently argued that his devotion to the ideals of democracy equals, if it does not surpass, that of his non-Jewish counterparts.

It should be added, however, that the refusal to regard the political ideal of one's adopted country as ultimate is a character not limited to the Jew. Other religious groups even in a democracy also refuse to recognize the national goal as supreme. Those, for example, who advocate a Christian democracy are asserting, in effect, that they do not perceive a nation which grants its citizens the right to practice a variety of creeds that are incompatible with Christianity as embodying what they would regard as their ultimate religious aspirations for society. The loyalty of the Jew is greater, by far, than that of those who espouse a sectarian democracy. The latter strive to transform the existing ideal, to change the character of the nation in which they reside, while the

Jew, though inspired by a vision of another day when the messianic era will introduce new political and social arrangements, in the meantime invests all his energy to preserve, defend, and strengthen political patterns associated with liberty.

Secondly, the Jew often attaches a different status to the political ideal of his adopted country than do many of his non-Jewish counterparts. If, for example, he lives in a democracy, his perspective on the significance of freedom will differ from that of many of his neighbors. It often happens that a political purpose is translated into an ethical end as well—for example, in a democracy, the ideal of liberty is, all too frequently, appropriated as the ultimate purpose of human life. If, moreover, freedom is interpreted in terms of doing whatever one is inclined to do, its adoption as the ethical goal tends to justify whatever impulses urge expression, so long as similar inclinations on the part of others are not frustrated. In the process, it is forgotten that freedom is essentially a political purpose, not an ethical goal. This, in large measure, has taken place in the United States. Americans have lost sight of the fact that the original American aim in projecting freedom as the nation's political goal was to assure its citizens the possibility of choosing a style of life or, if you will, a system of values projected by any one of a diversity of creeds. They fail to remember that the advantage of freedom as a political ideal is that it is a *means* which makes possible the choice of a variety of moral or religious ends. Since democracy allows the choice of freedom as the ethical goal of life, Americans opted in favor of expanding the significance of freedom so that it might become the ultimate in the scale of moral values as well.

It is otherwise with a *galut*-minded Jew. Since he is inspired by an ultimate political vision other than freedom—a vision that prescribes an ethical perspective in which freedom is not assigned the highest priority, he does not forget that freedom has essentially political significance and that it belongs to the category of means. He will devote himself, in an ambience of freedom, to the realization of values inherent in the Jewish ethical perspective. If he is a *galut*-conscious Jew, he will idealize, but not idolize, freedom. His is a healthier approach, insofar as his own life and the life of society are concerned, and, in addition, is more consistent with at least the original American conceptions.

It can be cogently argued that the idea of the melting pot emerged out of the transformation of freedom into an ethical goal, that is, out of the decision to treat liberty not merely as a means but as the ultimate purpose of human life. If the political objective is the creation of conditions in which a variety of creeds can be embodied in the lives of various segments of society, then any attempt to coerce all citizens into a common mold would have to be judged incompatible with the American ideal. If, however, freedom is perceived to give ethical meaning to life as well, then it is inevitable that the enterprise of recreating all citizens to exhibit in common the character of freedom would be undertaken. The greater popularity of pluralism in the United States today bears gratifying testimony to a deeper understanding of the nature of freedom among contemporary Americans.

Viewing freedom as a means also encourages the tendency to exhibit respect for those whose commitments we do not share. It is likely that those for whom freedom is the all-consuming passion in life will adopt a derogatory attitude towards any who refuse to be reshaped to conform to the mold fashioned by them. If, however, freedom is regarded, not as the ethical vision, but as that social and political arrangement in which a variety of ethical creeds may be selected, there is a greater probability of respect for one who exercises such freedom to choose criteria for conduct that differ from ours.

In addition, if freedom is construed as a means, individualism will not be pushed beyond the domain of its appropriate application. Individualism is one of the characteristic doctrines associated with freedom. In a democracy, an individual is granted the right to do as he wishes and to resist any pressures directed towards him by others. Unfortunately, the meaning of individualism has been expanded to include the notion that an individual must rely exclusively upon himself and that society is not responsible for improving the life of its citizens.

This interpretation has been used by many to relieve themselves of the duty to display concern for others. It has also been advanced by governments to press the claim that they have no obligation to assist those who are afflicted or deprived. Such a doctrine flows logically from a view which holds freedom to be not merely a political but an ethical ideal. Indeed, if individualism is applied as a principle in the ethical domain, then one citizen will not perceive himself as obligated to assist another in the pursuit of his well-being, though the life of the latter depends on it.

Judaism, on the other hand, while it recognizes the validity of individualism in a democratic context and advocates it, in many ways, in Jewish life, will not allow it to find application in a manner that would allow barriers of indifference to be erected between man and man. Nothing is more fundamental to Jewish life than the belief that we are responsible one for another. Such responsibility must be assumed in both the material and the spiritual realms. The *galut*-minded Jew is sensitive to his fellow man.

Finally, it should be added that the Jew, conscious of his *galut* status, assigns a different value to another American ideal, equality, than do others in the surrounding society. He understands and acknowledges the validity and importance of this basic political principle, but as noted in an earlier chapter, it is, to some extent at least, eclipsed by another principle, inequality. In other words, the Jew recognizes the occurrence of both equalities and inequalities in human beings. In the polling booth and before the bar of justice, all are equal, at least prescriptively; but by the standard of intellectual achievement, artistic talent, moral and religious conduct, inequality is the rule. The critical question is where the emphasis should be placed. The American will, very often, underscore common features, the Jew those that distinguish him. To the *galut* Jew, his Jewish and, therefore, differentiating characteristics are of the ultimate importance.

The result is an increase in tension between Jew and non-Jew. The non-Jew does not understand the customs of the Jew. The dietary laws are strange to him; the manner of the Jew's observance of the Sabbath is an enigma to him; the booths used on the festival of Sukkot are beyond his comprehension. What the non-

Jew understands even less, however, is the importance that these patterns of conduct have in the life of the Jew, that is, why the Jew does not pay greater attention to shared characteristics in order to cultivate closer relations with his fellow citizens rather than placing so much stress on separating features which tend to isolate him in the society to which he belongs.

There are thus two components in the reaction of a *galut*-conscious Jew to the principle of equality. One is a greater emphasis on distinguishing than on shared features; the second is a preference for differentiating characteristics even when they require his separation from others in the society to which he belongs. His historical thrust has been to be different and to preserve that difference; and if this attitude results in the erection of barriers between himself and the non-Jew—barriers that do not place limits to concern and compassion but to unrestrained social relationships and especially to intermarriages—the Jew understands this as the indispensable prerequisite for the preservation of Jewish life in the diaspora.

This attitude found its expression in the principle of *havdalah*, separation, which was applied, among other areas, to the relation of Jews to non-Jews. It was manifested in differences in conduct and even in dress. Separation was not merely a consequence of the decision to live as prescribed by the Torah; it was, in addition, an explicit principle which pervaded the Jewish mind and which emphasized the Jewish demand that priority be assigned to Jewish over non-Jewish patterns of living.[3] Such an attitude, though it is compatible with mutual respect, advocates separation and, as a result, introduces tension into the relationship of Jews and non-Jews. The *galut* Jew inevitably experienced political strains in the society in which he lived.

II

A positive aspect of the *galut* mentality is the extraordinary unity it introduced into a dispersed Jewish community. Indeed, the sense of sharing life in exile forged an inseverable bond between Jew and Jew.

It is important to note that the sense of *galut* is not the feeling that I alone am in exile but that I belong to an exiled community whose characteristic conditions, in virtue of my membership in it, I inevitably share. The sense of exile is, therefore, simultaneously a sense of community.

Unity, generally, derives from a variety of factors; one of these is the feeling by a group's members that they share the same fate and destiny. Both of these—the sense of fate and the sense of destiny—are powerful galvanizing forces in the life of a people. They are indispensable for the achievement of unity when a people is without a homeland and dispersed among the nations of the world. If a people occupies a common territorial location—the normal condition among nations—its sense of unity flows from a shared geography and purpose. When the normal circumstances of national life are not present, it needs something much more powerful to unite it. The Jew finds it in the consciousness of being in *galut*.

A sense of fate or destiny or both is a defining component of the *galut* mentality. The sense of fate is the conviction that the anguish and travail of the Jew in the world is inevitable and, to one degree or another, inescapable. He may live in a democracy in which freedom and equality are constitutionally guaranteed, yet he or a member of his family will, at some time, become a target of anti-Semitism, in explicit or subtle form. The attempt continues to be made, by thoughtful and perceptive scholars, to go beyond the symptoms and to identify the roots of this social disease, but it is consistently unsuccessful. Religious, economic, political, racial bases of this affliction have been uncovered and carefully analyzed, but we have no greater insight into the germs, so deadly in nature and so devastating in results, than ever before. It would almost appear that anti-Semitism is an ineradicable historic phenomenon. In the Jewish community, it is often interpreted in terms of a Jewish fate.

The fate of the Jew has also been characterized in theological terms. In the Bible, pain and suffering are often justified in terms of their pedagogical value rather than as punishment. "And He afflicted you and made you hungry . . . that He might teach you that man does not live by bread alone, but by every thing that proceeds from the mouth of God does man live."[4] The prophet Isaiah often refers to the *eved ha-Shem*, the servant of God, who, according to many commentators, is identified with the people of Israel. It is the fate of this servant to suffer even while he experiences unqualified faith in God. "I gave my back to the smiters, and my cheeks to them that plucked off the hair; I hid not my face from shame and spitting. For the Lord God helped me; therefore have I not been confounded."[5] This prophetic portrait of the servant of God, who symbolized the fate of the people of Israel, provided the theological basis, not merely for resignation in the face of Jewish suffering, but for the view that such suffering is of inestimable value and indispensable to the cultivation of a people of great character and extraordinary spiritual quality. The Jew's perception of his own fate thus found its rationale, not in mere historical conditions, but in a transcendental source.

In addition to the sense of Jewish fate, there was also, in the Jewish community, a sense of Jewish destiny. The Jew perceived in the very existence of the Jewish people a divine or, at the very least, a transcendental purpose which helped to shape Jewish history. To the religious mind, this destiny informed the process, in which the Jewish people was to take an indispensable part, of bringing to realization the messianic era. To the secular Jewish mind, a transnatural purpose, which he could not define precisely, gave the Jew a very special character. One scholar formulated the sense of destiny of the secular Jew in just such terms. In responding to the question, "Of what does Jewish identity consist to the adherent of civil Judaism?" he wrote,

> The traditional Judaic theological concept which seems to me to provide the keynote in civil Jewish faith is the concept of Jewish chosenness. This concept is not always articulated openly or explicitly. But the sense of "mission" and "destiny" which filters throughout civil Judaism has, as far as I can tell, no other grounding. . . . In the civil Jewish religious system, chosenness essentially means Jewish distinctiveness and Jewish service—but it gives these a transcendental basis.[6]

The important thing to note, insofar as our discussion is concerned, is that the unity introduced into the community by a sense of fate and destiny differs dramatically from that which is achieved through a social purpose. In the first place, the latter variety is often derived from considerations of self-interest. The social contract, as has been noted frequently in these pages, provides the theoretical basis for democracy. The general thrust of its arguments is that a citizen is prepared to assume obligations only if he is adequately supplied with a compensatory quantity of rights. He is prepared to invest his energies on behalf of freedom, for himself as well as for others, because of the rewards it will ultimately yield for him. To the Jew with a sense of fate and destiny, concern with self is irrelevant to his relations to others in the Jewish community. He believes himself to be carried along, in virtue of his membership in that community, by transcendental forces. The unity of the Jewish community is essentially of the unselfish variety.

Secondly, the unity that is rooted in the sense of fate and destiny has an emotional character that is derived from a feeling of identity with others in the community. The belief that what happens to the totality will happen to each in virtue of his membership in the same community of fate welds one Jew to another with an invisible but powerful link of feeling that is not easily broken. The sense that their lives are, at least partially, controlled by the same transcendent purpose instills into the relationship of Jew and Jew a sense of partnership and sharing that strengthens the identification of each with the other. This is not to say that the relation of citizen to citizen in a society whose unity is dependent on a common conception of a social purpose is not tinged with emotion. It certainly is; but the emotional element is essentially derivative and a by-product of the commitment to pursue a common social aim. It spills over from a feeling about freedom to an attachment to those who share a devotion to freedom. The empathy of Jew for Jew, however, is not primarily a function of a commitment to a common cause—though this too is included in the schema of interrelationships in the Jewish community—but of an identification that results from the conviction that the fate and destiny of one Jew is intricately interwoven with those of his compatriots. The emotional attachment is, for that very reason, deeper and stronger.

Finally, the unity that is based on commitment to a common social aim is collective in character, while, at least ideally, the unity associated with a sense of shared fate and destiny is organic in nature. One might initially indicate the difference between these two forms of unity by example. An army possesses a collective unity, while the unity of a single human being is organic. A man also consists of parts, but these parts have a closer relationship to each other than do soldiers in an army. Organic unity expresses itself in two ways: (1) when one part of the organism is in pain—for example, a severe headache—the entire organism suffers; and (2) if one part of the organism commits a transgression—for example, the hand steals—the entire organism is responsible. The rabbis of the Talmud declared that these two characteristics are applicable to the Jewish people. Each Jew is obligated to share the pain experienced by his fellow Jews;[7] and each Jew is responsible for the violations of Torah precepts on the part of others in the Jewish community, that is, "all Jews are responsible one for another."[8] Obviously, the sense of a shared fate and destiny increases the possibility of achieving an organic unity for the Jewish people.

III

The sense of *galut* also supplies the impetus for Jews in the diaspora to undertake initiatives to eliminate the condition of exile and to restore their sovereignty in their historic homeland. It is an indisputable fact that this sense was instrumental to the emergence of the Zionist movement in the nineteenth century and to the rebirth of the modern State of Israel. The important question is whether, now that the State of Israel has been reestablished, it makes any sense, in terms of the political status of the Jewish people, to speak of it as still in *galut?* If it does, the struggle for political redemption is not yet at an end, and the concept of *galut* still has a critical role to play. If it does not, this concept becomes a historical relic.

It is obvious that the attitudes towards exile on the part of the religious and nonreligious segments of the Jewish community differ. Secular-minded *galut*-conscious Jews are satisfied with the achievement of political independence, a condition in which the destiny of the Jewish people, which they are not able to define but in which they firmly believe, can be realized. Those who are motivated by religious considerations define Jewish destiny, at a minimum, in terms of the reshaping of the social and political structure of the Jewish nation to conform with the requirements of Torah. Secular Jews can continue to speak of living in *galut* simultaneously with the existence of a Jewish state only if they live beyond its boundaries. If they find themselves within the state, they inevitably perceive themselves as redeemed. If they believe in some transcendent purpose, they cannot know whether it has been achieved and hence cannot define the concept of *galut* in terms of its absence. For the religious Jew, however, it makes sense to speak of *galut* even in the present era and for the resident of the Holy Land. From his perspective, *galut* means, not only the absence of a politically independent state, but also an existing state with a political structure that does not reflect the requirements of Torah. Hence, even in the era of the reborn State of Israel, the religious Jew cannot entirely escape the feeling that he and the people to which he belongs are still in *galut*. As the prayer on behalf of Israel formulated by the Chief Rabbinate puts it, the contemporary state is only "the beginning of our redemption." This qualification is to be understood in a political sense as well.

The laws of the State of Israel do not embody biblical and rabbinic precepts. Even the laws of personal status, which do reflect the requirements of traditional Judaism, were introduced for sociological reasons, not because they are prescribed by religious principle. The personalities who are charged with governing the state are, by and large, nonreligious Jews, at least in the classic Jewish sense. To the religious Jewish mind, this situation, while it is a considerable improvement, is not entirely satisfactory. The religious Jew has not yet emerged from the *galut* condition; he continues to face the task of mounting a program to achieve redemption.

IV

Galut is a concept that, when integrated into the human personality, instills an attitude that is powerful in its thrust. Even while, historically, the sense of *galut* introduced tension into the relations of Jews and non-Jews, it also frequently, galvanized the Jewish people into concerted action and made available to it the energy needed to bring into existence the modern State of Israel.

14

Social Policy

Since we will be concerned with methodology in relation to social policy, a few general remarks on the concept of method are appropriate at the start. This concept is generic, applicable equally to logic, mathematics, science, art, theology, and other areas of human experience. Some aspects of a specific method are characteristic of the discipline for which it was invented; others are general. The general elements find exemplification in the theological enterprise of formulating and implementing social policy as much as they do in the mathematical process of deducing theorems from axioms and the scientific procedure of verifying hypotheses about the universe on the basis of experimentation.

There are four elements that seem to be essential determinants of method in any human venture. The first and, I believe, the most important is the goal to be achieved. If we seek to extract meanings that may be hidden in a set of statements, the method of logical deduction is suitable. If we aim for knowledge of the empirical universe, observation and experimentation seem to be the appropriate means. The method chosen flows somehow from the end to be attained. Second, assumptions often play a crucial role in the selection of a method. One recalls, for example, the era of rationalism, when it was assumed that the mind could, out of its own contents, extract truths about the universe, and when observation was regarded as a source of deception and error.

Scientific method then differed from what it is today, a difference that was ultimately derived from diverse epistemological assumptions concerning the best approach to the acquisition of truth. To the extent that theology is not a domain accessible to empirical procedures, the role of assumption in the determination of its methodology may be considerable. Third, success in achieving the contemplated goal is a crucial factor in the validation of a proposed method. This is an obvious requirement. The very definition of method implies that it is an *instrument* for the realization of an objective. If that objective is not attained, the means intended to accomplish it can hardly be elevated to the status of method. Finally, a method must somehow take into account present circumstances. I recall reading a description by a well-known artist of the methods he employs in his work, in which he declared that his brush stroke is determined not merely by his conception of the total painting he intends to produce but even more so by the concatenation of colors present at the moment he applies his brush to the canvas. In any case, it is evident that method must take into account the materials available at any given time and introduce procedures for manipulating them in a way that will bring the individual or society closer to the attainment of the designated objectives.

I

All four elements of method are present in the formulation and implementation of Jewish social policy. Of paramount importance is the goal to be achieved. The goal that Judaism projects as the highest good, the *summum bonum*, is the introduction of sanctity into human life—the life of the individual, the family, and the community. The concept of sanctity may of course be interpreted in a variety of ways. Some take it to apply primarily to certain rituals practiced by a religious community. It is interpreted, alternatively, as relevant only to principles of morality. There are those who denigrate ritual in comparison with moral conduct and believe that the sacred is only to be found in human relations when human behavior is guided and inspired by moral rules. Even on this interpretation, however, there is a vast difference between reducing the sacred to the moral and elevating the moral to the sacred. If the sacred is, among other things, that which has its source in the divine will, then the identification of the moral and the sacred is a declaration that moral principle has a divine source. The moral accordingly undergoes an elevation. If, on the other hand, as Immanuel Kant suggested, the holy will is one whose actions are determined purely by practical reason in conformity to the categorical imperative, that is, the voice of conscience, there is a reduction of the sacred to the moral. For the saintly individual, according to this conception, does not respond to the will of God but to a moral conscience to which an atheist may equally respond and claim for himself an identical degree of sanctity.

From the Jewish vantage point, therefore, whether the holy is that which characterizes ritualistic procedures or moral principles or both, an essential feature of the sacred turns out to be its divine origin. The goal of the sacred, even when it is interpreted as a character of the moral, should then be construed in terms of the human response to the divine will.

Now, the view that the introduction of sanctity into human life is the goal of Jewish social policy implies that it is essential to create institutions in which the sense of the sacred can be communicated effectively—hence, the emphasis in Judaism on the enterprise of education. Education is a means and perhaps the best means for instilling a sense of the sacred into the human personality. The hope is that if the experience of the sacred is transmitted successfully, it will spill over into the larger community.

It is essential to add that the Jewish educational process, in its classic form, focuses on action rather than information. The cardinal category of the Jewish religion is not the principle but the precept, the *mitzvah*. Its thrust is not so much theoretical, that is, to teach what we shall believe, as it is practical, to exhibit what we must do in response to the will of God. The author of a great rabbinic work explains the reason for it.

Know then that the human being is molded in conformity to his actions, whether good or evil. If a thorough scoundrel whose early thoughts are entirely evil will arouse his spirit and will strive and engage constantly in the study of Torah and the performance of commandments, though not for the sake of Heaven, he will soon turn to the good and with the power of his deeds destroy the evil inclination. For the heart is drawn after deeds.[1]

This discussion is crucial to the question of the formulation and implementation of social policy. Fundamentally, two approaches to the solution of social problems are possible. One is sociological. Society's social structure can be transformed in such a way that the impact of specific problems may be reduced or even eradicated. This might be done by the restructuring of old institutions or the introduction of new ones. The other is moral. Alternatively, the individual members of society, through a process of education, may undergo changes in character which could also lead to the same result. If, for example, society is afflicted by theft or greed, one may propose the abolition of private property. In the absence of the possibility of material possessions, one could not take title to that which belongs to another, that is, one could not steal, and, further, in such a social context, greed would not be a very useful sentiment. This would represent a sociological solution. Or, one may attempt to instill within the members of society a sense of honesty and generosity of spirit together with an appreciation of the sacred dimension of these moral virtues. This is a moral solution. It focuses on change in individual character rather than on the transformation of institutions. Private property could then be preserved, but theft and greed would be severely diminished. The enterprise of education is indispensable to the second alternative, which, indeed, is central to Jewish methodology. In fact, Judaism seeks to create a religio-ethical society through that form of education that stresses action.

One important consequence of Judaism's emphasis on the practical form of education is that the family becomes the crucial instrument in the process that leads to the cultivation of the sense of the sacred. The burden of education does not belong exclusively to the school. It must be carried by the family as well, which, on the Jewish view, must even assume the greater share. The school will fulfill the purpose of the communication of knowledge and provide the explanation, even the justification, of principles. But the practice of precepts must be prompted and supervised in the home and by parents. Respect for parents, for example, cannot be assured by class discussion. It is necessary that children be taught to practice the precepts of conduct into which the principle of respect is translated and which have the capacity to instill the attitude of respect into the hearts of the young. When children are trained to avoid sitting on seats reserved for a parent, to refain from contradicting parents, never to respond to a parent with abuse, they learn, in practice, that sense of reverence that constitutes respect for a parent. Similarly, if the charitable inclination is cultivated by *acts* of generosity, parents cannot leave it to the school to instill kindness and unselfishness into their children. They must themselves supervise their children in the performance of such acts. It is for this reason that the primary responsibility for teaching children the Torah was placed on the parent. Hence, the family, because it is the most effective means in the task of developing moral character among its members, is indispensable to the resolution of those social problems accessible to moral solution.

But Judaism, even while it adopts the moral approach, does not repudiate the sociological approach. Hence, and in the second place, Jewish social policy requires that the Jewish community shall advocate, in society in general, the creation of institutions that will enhance the status of the sacred and the enactment of legislation that will permit the existence and growth of commitment to that which is sanctioned by the sacred. Judaism places a great deal of emphasis on the need to live in a community in which the patterns of public conduct enforce rather than negate moral and religious attitudes. Thus it is judged desirable to avoid living in a city where certain institutions are not available, for example, judicial and penal institutions for the purpose of enforcing the moral code, charitable agencies to assist those in need, a synagogue, a school, and so on.[2]

Judaism would even allow change and experimentation with

social institutions whose existence is assumed and implicitly sanctioned in the Bible. In the religious kibbutzim in Israel, for example, principles of modern socialism have been appropriated and elevated into the realm of the sacred by relating them to the biblical principle of justice. Rabbis have defended this innovation on the grounds that, even while the principles of socialism are not imposed as obligations by biblical and rabbinic traditions—the system of capitalism is clearly sanctioned—they do nevertheless represent a fulfillment of the requirements of justice, Jewishly conceived. Judaism would then allow experimentation and innovation in social patterns and relations in order to get closer to the realization of the ideal of justice in society. It is clear that while Judaism may focus on the individual and his moral development, it also strives to bring into being the kind of social structure that will facilitate the fulfillment of those moral principles advocated and sanctioned by Him who is the Source of the sacred.

But Judaism takes a further step. Where it is not incompatible with the preservation of genuine religious pluralism in our country, it would endorse legislation that will have the effect of encouraging the creation and the growth of institutions devoted to the achievement of the sacred. The separation of church and state is a political, not a religious, principle. Indeed, with Judaism itself, the political and the religious are inseparable; the city of man is incorporated into the city of God. Notwithstanding, Judaism must always take into account the political climate in which it finds itself to assure the preservation of religious freedom. Further, there is a rabbinic precept which declares, "the law of the land is the law." Where a state in which Jews live prescribes that its citizens shall conduct themselves according to certain rules, and, further, where these rules do not prevent Jews from fulfilling their religious obligation, they are required to obey them. Hence, Jews seek to respond positively and constructively to the separation of the religious from the political in American life. It is sometimes necessary to do so and, in any case, it is the law of the land. There is a problem, of course, with regard to the extent of such separation, but this is a political, not a religious, issue. Its solution must be undertaken, not by Judaism and in conformity to its religious requirements, but by American democracy and in harmony with its understanding of the meaning of its Constitution. Americans with religious commitments will, of course, share in the political debate. But however the problem may ultimately be resolved by Congress and the Supreme Court, the result will be acceptable to Judaism because it has adopted the rabbinic principle that "the law of the land is the law."[3] In any event, when a proposed law or a new American institution holds promise of enhancing the domain of the sacred, and where religious pluralism is not threatened by it, it will be judged deserving of support.

In addition, Judaism will urge social legislation that will contribute to the achievement of social aims that are endorsed by the sacred. Laws intended to ease the pain of those oppressed or in anguish may be interpreted as consistent with the requirements of mercy or justice or both and, in any case, if enacted would create social conditions in which these religious ideals would receive implementation. Judaism would advocate such procedures, sanction them as acceptable social policies, and applaud their application to society.

II

In truth, the methodological principles discussed thus far flow not merely from the objectives that the methods to be chosen are intended to realize, but also from certain assumptions that Judaism makes with regard to the nature of man and society. This leads to the second important general determinant of method, namely, the assumptions adopted.

The first Jewish postulate that deserves attention is that the human being has an almost unlimited potential for spiritual development. As Maimonides puts it, "Every man has the capacity to be as righteous as Moses or, for that matter, as evil as Jeroboam."[4] Granted that this is the case, it will not do merely to manipulate social pattterns, that is, to restructure institutions in order to achieve intended social objectives. It is also important, via the school, the synagogue, and above all, the family, to mold personalities whose moral commitments will ultimately be reflected in social relations.

But, further, on the Jewish view, it is even more important. Greater emphasis is placed by Judaism on the building of moral character than on the creation of new institutional forms. This may be inferred from the fact that Judaism's system of religion is formulated in terms of precepts of conduct addressed to the members of the community rather than in terms of the portrayal of ideals to be achieved or detailed accounts of desirable economic, social, and political institutions to be created. The emphasis upon ideals and institutions alone, at least in the social arena, could have led to the conclusion that the way to realize Judaism's social aims is by means of sociological transformation alone. Judaism's self-definition in terms of commandments means that even the realization of the social objective is ultimately dependent on the development of moral character. Hence, the *mitzvot* are also frequently enunciated in the singular. The commandments are directed at the individual human personality. Hence too, the ends to be achieved through the practice of the commandments remain essentially tacit and unspoken. Judaism appears to have opted in favor of the formulation of a method, confident that if the right method will be employed, the desired goal will ultimately be attained.

There is a second postulate of Jewish thought relevant to our theme. Patterns of individual behavior and social relations which conform to Judaism's requirements, though they are not motivated by religious commitments, are also of value. One rabbinic commentary, for example, declares, "Would that were they to reject Me, they would at least observe my commandments."[5] The rationale for this judgment is that *mitokh she-lo li-shemah, bo li-shemah*, those who observe the commandments for ulterior motives may eventually cultivate genuine religious commitments. In any case, there is value in the adoption of the moral and social objectives of Jewish life on a nonreligious basis and pursuing them without any recognition of the dimension of the sacred that attaches to them. There is much in Torah that could be chosen on utilitarian grounds alone as conducive to man's well-being and his happiness. It is Judaism's view that a choice for pragmatic reasons may ultimately lead to genuine commitment.

III

There is a third determinant of method, namely, success. In a sense, it is the most important one, because a method that does not lead to the intended objective hardly deserves to be entitled a method. Success is the touchstone of methodology. The crucial question, however, is: what are the criteria of success?

It may be argued that, in the religious arena, successful methodology produces desirable results in the transcendental domain, that is to say, an action in the realm of nature is to be viewed not merely in the category of a cause with empirical consequences in the form of effects but also as producing certain results in a more important spiritual domain in comparison with which that which happens here and now is relatively trivial. If this view were adopted, the success of religious methodology could be tested only by the extent to which the actions of men in society reflect religious prescriptions. Their social implications would not be material. While there are rabbinic interpreters of Judaism who direct attention to the spiritual nexus in which human actions are involved, their social consequences are, nevertheless, deemed to be of paramount importance. Indeed, assuring justice for those who are exploited, providing sustenance to the impoverished and healing to the sick are spiritual actions of the highest magnitude. Hence, the Jewish criterion for the success of the methodology aimed at social policy is essentially empirical and quantifiable.

That criterion has two elements. Success is measured by (1) the degree to which social institutions impose effective constraints upon society's members so that their social conduct will embody religious values, and (2) the degree to which individuals are motivated to conduct themselves in accord with those moral principles that lead to social arrangements sanctioned by Judaism. The first element will not, by itself, suffice. There are occasions when institutional constraints are weak, inadequate, or altogether absent. The international political arena offers a perennial example. The United Nations and other international bodies are not very effective in preventing the perpetration of injustice by one nation upon another. There are societies in which portions of the population are excluded from human compassion and the protection of the law. Such, for example, was the Jewish people under Nazi dominion. A blackout in an American city often has the effect of leaving individuals and their property at the mercy of criminal impulses. When institutional constraints are removed, the social structure may break down, and violence, looting, and theft may become the order of the day—unless individual conscience were sufficiently developed morally to prevent it. This is the Jewish objective. The success of social policy, insofar as Judaism is concerned, must be measured, among other things, by the extent to which moral principles are integrated into the human personality.

IV

The final determinant of method is the character of the present. Prevailing conditions often dictate the means that must be employed to accomplish a specific aim. This applies to both enterprises—the sociological and the moral.

In the nineteenth century, for example, when rugged individualism went almost unchallenged, the sociological method that could be utilized to provide every human being with the minimum of goods necessary for survival differed radically from that which could best be employed in the twentieth century, in which the goal of individual security is pursued by government-sponsored social programs. What had to be done by means of voluntary institutions supported by philanthropic endeavors in the earlier period can now be accomplished by federal and state legislation. The methods of yesterday differ from those of today as do the institutions of charity from those of government.

Now, while the task of formulating and implementing social policies intended to arrange social patterns so that their human consequences will coincide with Jewish ideals is less difficult today than it was in the past, the reverse is true with those social policies whose purpose it is to mold moral character. In an era in which religious commitment is widespread, the task of communicating it is less difficult. It may even be accomplished by instruction because existing community forces encourage, support, and strengthen the religious posture. In a secular and amoral society, on the other hand, the task is incredibly more difficult. The methods of instilling commitment in a social context in which, by virtue of prevalent social forces, such commitments, even where they are present, are constantly suffering erosion have not been adequately established. It may perhaps be accomplished by the building of communities, pockets of religious life, in which moral character with the capacity to resist the winds of doctrine and the morally destructive attitudes available in the marketplace may be developed. But it is obvious that the task is enormous and the methods different.

V

The sociological approach to social policy is much more popular today than is the moral. There are several reasons for this. One of these is the rejection of religious values because of the climate of secularism in which we live, and the repudiation of traditional moral norms because they do not find support in the universe of facts to the study of which science is dedicated. This circumstance renders the task of religion all the more difficult. But, insofar as Judaism is concerned, there is no adequate substitute for the moral approach to the formulation and implementation of social policy.

15

Revolution

Revolution as a means of effecting social change is often advocated; the concept calls for analysis. While revolution has many aspects, historical, psychological, and so forth, its moral aspects will occupy our attention here. We will be concerned with the problem of justification. Under what circumstances, if any, is the revolutionary enterprise justified?

I

The term *revolution* is used ambiguously in the literature of the subject; it is necessary to define it—at least we must state the way in which we intend to use the term. In a general way, and at the start, we may identify as a revolution a series of events that have as a consequence the transformation of the social and political structure of a society. A more detailed characterization of the idea of revolution reveals that it contains three ingredients.

First, it includes the element of social progress. It is this aspect that is contemplated when historians and social theorists refer with admiration and approval to the series of events that are designated today, the American, the French, or the Russian Revolution. Progress has been construed as a greater freedom in a political sense (as in the case of the American Revolution) and/or an improvement in the quality of life (as in the cases of the French and Russian Revolutions).

Obviously, a mere social-political transformation of society does not in itself constitute progress. The change may be retrogressive rather than progressive. History supplies numerous examples of societies in which political and social relations went through extensive alterations which were not subsequently identified as revolutionary; for example, the substitution, in Germany, of a fascist for a democratic state. This event was not counted as a revolution because the element of progress, that is, an increase in freedom or an improvement in the quality of life, was absent.

A very important conclusion may be drawn immediately. The attempt to justify revolution on the grounds that it has always resulted in progress is not legitimate. The reason that revolutions are associated with progress is that a social-political transformation whose outcome has not been a step in the forward direction has never been labeled a revolution.

The second ingredient in the concept of revolution is *extensive* change in the social and political system. Hannah Arendt speaks of revolutionary change as that which involves a new beginning and novelty.[1] Others describe this type of change as fundamental. I believe, however, that it is the element of extensive change that is characteristic.

A society usually justifies its existence and validates its institutions by means of a theory. When the theory is made explicit, it is an ideology. (This should not be taken to mean that the character of any society in fact exemplifies, in every detail, the ideology to which it is verbally committed. This is rarely, if ever, the case.) A revolution may take place in *theory*; for example, a specific ideology may be proposed as preferable to another—democracy instead of monarchy, let us say. Even before changes in social *fact* have occurred, the theory is labeled revolutionary. If we construe the theory of monarchy as a logical system (which it is not) beginning with axioms and proceeding to the theorems that these axioms imply, then it may be said that the theory of democracy introduces *fundamental* changes or that it involves *a new beginning* in that it rejects some of the axioms of the monarchial theory and puts others in their place. But when we deal with the social *fact* of change, we are hard put to find a characterization of *fundamental* and *new beginning* that is similar to what we find in the case of theory. Which social fact, for example, or what social institution is the counterpart of an axiom?

It may be observed, however, that an axiom may be taken to be fundamental, not because it happens to stand at the base of a logical system, but because so much of the system depends on it. If one axiom is replaced by another, the consequences of the change are felt throughout the system. The change is extensive. This notion is applicable to social fact as well. Transformations in certain social facts have practical implications in wide areas of social and political experience. The Supreme Court decision ruling that segregation was unconstitutional is a good example of this ingredient in the concept of revolution. It has been regarded as revolutionary because, it was believed, the changes it would ultimately bring about were sure to be widespread.

The third element in the concept of revolution is violence. Whether violence should or should not be included in the definition of *revolution* is, in fact, debated in the literature. Even Marx's views on revolution have been subjected to contrary interpretations. At this point, suffice it to observe that it is precisely the inclusion of violence in the concept of revolution that renders the question of the morality of revolution problematic. If widespread social progress could be effected without bringing repression, injury, or death to society's members, and if this were the revolutionary's intensions, the question of justification would hardly be raised. The moral issue is urgent because violence is normally included in the revolutionary's conception of his enterprise.

It will be useful to identify that aspect of violent behavior with which we shall be primarily concerned. Destroying property, inflicting injury, committing suicide are also forms of violence that raise crucial moral issues. In this discussion, however, we will address ourselves only to the morality of those actions that consciously endanger the lives of others. These are the most extreme of the forms of behavior that advocates of revolution attempt to justify. It is also a criticism of this attempt that reveals most clearly some dubious aspects of the revolutionary's assumptions.

It will also be appropriate, at this point, to distinguish two different motivations for violence. In one case, violence is a response to the experience of frustration and despair. It appears as an inevitable and uncontrollable eruption because of existing social conditions. It occurs without plan or premeditation. In the second case, violence is suggested as an activity resulting from deliberation and choice. It is urged as the rational application of a method designed to bring about certain desirable results. In the first instance, the moral task is one of *evaluating* behavior which is construed as determined by the laws of social causality. In the second case, the moral concern is one of *obligating* behavior that is regarded as essential to the realization of a social objective. Since violence has been urged in the revolutionary program as a matter of obligation, and because this is the strongest form of moral sanction that violent activity has received, our attention will be directed to this aspect of the moral issue.

II

We will consider one representative attempt at justifying violence in the revolutionary process. The argument includes the main features in the reasoning of those who attempt to supply moral sanction to the method of violence. The following summarizes the views of H. Marcuse as they are developed in his essay "Ethics and Revolution."[2]

1. It is the purpose of government to assure the members of society the enjoyment of freedom and happiness. Happiness is defined as "a life without fear and misery, and a life in peace." Later in the essay, it is claimed that such a life is dependent upon the widest distributions of goods produced in the process of developing available material and human resources.

2. Freedom and happiness are never *fully* realized in any society at any point of its historical development. Every society, in virtue of its social and political structure, subjects its members to repression and violence. No matter, therefore, the extent of any society's advance in the direction of realizing its social aims, it

always falls short. For some segment of the population and, in some ways, for the entire population, freedom or happiness is lacking.

3. Violence that is part of the revolutionary process is counterviolence. In the Reign of Terror, for example, "violence, revolutionary violence, appears not only as political means but as moral duty. The terror is defined as *counter* violence: it is 'legitimate' only in defense against oppressors and until they are defeated."

4. It is possible to calculate the social consequence of the revolutionary process. An inventory may be made of the human and material resources available to a society and of its facilities of production and distribution. It is also possible to calculate the extent to which more goods would become available and to a larger segment of society if the revolutionary proposal were put into effect. Such a calculation may exhibit the proposed society envisioned by the revolutionaries as the better one.

> Calculable are the material and intellectual resources available, calculable are the productive and distributive facilities in a society, and the extent of unsatisfied vital needs and of satisfied nonvital needs. Quantifiable and calculable are the quantity and size of the labor force and of the population as a whole. . . . And on the basis of the quantifiable material the question can be asked whether the available resources and capabilities are utilized . . . with a view to the best possible satisfaction of needs. . . . If the analysis . . . suggests a negative answer . . . then the reversal of such conditions . . . would also be a maximalization of the chance of progress in freedom. Consequently, a social and political movement in this direction would, in terms of the calculus, allow the presumption of historical justification.

5. Violence is indispensable as a method of realizing the better society, "Non-violent history is the promise and possibility of a society which is still to be fought for." There is no alternative to violence.

REVOLUTION   181

6. Hence violence is justified in a revolutionary program.

The claims set forth in paragraphs 1 and 2 may be granted. One can of course take issue with the conception of happiness formulated here or debate the extent to which freedom and happiness are, in fact, exemplified in a specific society at some historic point. But these issues are not relevant to our central concern, namely, the morality of violence in a revolutionary struggle.

Attention, therefore, will be directed to the claims and presuppositions of paragraphs 3, 4, and 5.

III

What kind of violence justifies the use of counterviolence? Judaism provides a relatively clear answer. We are concerned here with the talmudic category of the *rodef*, the assailant who pursues with the intention to kill. Judaism declares that not only the pursued but the bystander as well is obligated to prevent the murder, even if it is necessary to make use of violence in the process. But what is the nature of an act of violence that justifies the use of counterviolence? First, the assailant's act must be one that could result in death. If its possible consequences are limited to depriving another of a property right or economic opportunity, the sort of counterviolence that would result in the death of the assailant is prohibited. The Talmud makes it clear that one may not kill a thief if it is certain that the thief will not, under any circumstances, attempt to kill his intended victim if the latter should resist the theft.[3] Second, it must be the assailant's intention to commit murder. If the intention is lacking, though the threat and danger to life are clear and present, counterviolence is not indicated. The Talmud declares that if a mother's life is threatened by an infant not yet fully emerged from the womb, but already at the stage where his individuality is legally recognized, the infant may not be dismembered in the attempt to save the mother, because no intention to murder is present.[4] One commentator summed up these two conditions in his definition of a *rodef* as "one who intends to inflict upon his neighbor an injury that results in death."[5]

The Talmud also deals with the range of justifiable counter-violence. First, an act of counterviolence may not be excessive. Death may not be inflicted when an injury will suffice to overcome the assailant. "If it is possible to save the intended victim by maiming the assailant, he is not permitted to kill."[6] Second, counter-violence is justifiable only when pursuit is taking place. If there is no immediate threat to life—for example, the assailant has temporarily retreated—there is no further ground for counterviolence. Thus, "If the thief (who came by stealth, prepared to kill if necessary) retired from the house, he is no longer identified as an assailant."[7]

The discussion, so far, centers on the relation of violence among individuals. What concerns us even more, however, is the role of violence in an individual's response to society. Suppose the society in question is characterized by a system of laws, with institutions to implement them, which prescribe the annihilation of a specific community. We may then characterize the society and its institutions as violent. What principles guide the use of counterviolence in such a case?

It is reasonable to assume that the principles that are relevant to individuals are applicable here too. Variations occur mainly in the applications of these principles because of differences in context. These contextual differences are, of course, crucial. In the case of the individual, the agent generally acts without the co-operation of others and in contradiction to the accepted social scheme of things. Social conditions support the intended victim rather than the assailant. There are obstacles to the performance of the act other than that the pursued may rise in his own defense. When society is violent, the act of murder turns out to be a co-operative venture and existing conditions support the assailants rather than their targets. Those engaged in the violent enterprise need not, for example, be concerned with social retribution or ostracism. These differences, however, do not render the principles that set limits to counterviolence irrelevant; they merely make their application more difficult.

There are, for example, important differences in the application of the principles that limit the violent response. It is relatively easy, in the case of the individual, to identify the moment when an assailant has stopped pursuing his victim. Can this be done in the case where violence is a cooperative venture prescribed by law and implemented by institutions? Suppose that none of society's agents is, *at the moment*, hunting for a victim, has the society ceased to be violent? And what, in the social matrix, is the counterpart of the requirement that counterviolence shall be minimal, that is, that no more be applied than that quantity which is sufficient to render the enemy harmless? Setting boundaries to counterviolence is clearly more difficult in the social arena.

But there are more important differences. In the case of an individual, the identification of the enemy, that is, the would-be assailant, is relatively simple. He is either directing a deadly weapon at his victim or is performing an act which, if successful, brings death immediately and inevitably. But who, in the social context, should be designated an assailant? An ancient midrashic illustration will serve the purpose of clarification. The citizens of Sodom were guided by certain laws relating to strangers. If an alien entered the city, he was not permitted to leave, and while citizens were encouraged to contribute in a monetary way, none was allowed either to give or sell him any food. A visit inevitably resulted in death. Who, in this case, is the enemy? Is it the legislators who enacted the laws, the storekeepers who refused to sell the visitor any food, the guards who prevented him from leaving? How about the citizen who, aware of such goings-on, did nothing about them?

Further, in the case of the individual, the intent to kill is either verbally explicit or clear from the act itself. The assailant is never silent. On the other hand, an inactive or indifferent spectator is never an appropriate target for counterviolence. The latter is a scoundrel, on the Jewish view. He has failed to abide by the precept which prohibits silence in the presence of murder.[8] But retaliation by violence for silence is not condoned. What of a silent spectator in a society which has legislated the extermination of a minority community? Is the person who is aware of, but declines to object to, the violence prescribed by the legal system a silent partner in the enterprise of murder?

These questions point to some of the difficulties involved in applying the principles that justify counterviolence to the social sphere, but these principles remain valid for that domain nevertheless. If this is granted, several important consequences follow. First, one may not, on the Jewish view and on the grounds of counterviolence, attack with intent to kill those who are not the enemy. In a social order which does not consciously *prescribe* the physical annihilation of a group of people, no one may be regarded as an enemy, deserving of counterviolence, if he has not, in his individual behavior, combined action and intent in the attempt to kill.

An instance of violence in a society—for example, the starvation of an individual—is usually the result of a variety of actions of whose implications their authors are hardly aware and whose consequences they do not intend. Such events, in general, flow from the concomitance of a number of factors each of which is associated with a different individual who, because he is unaware of the other causal conditions, cannot anticipate and certainly does not intend the violent results. The executive who fails to employ a hungry man, whose life subsequently ends in starvation, normally does not know that the victim's family refused him assistance and his community denied him charity. The principle of counterviolence, on the Jewish view, cannot legitimatize violence towards people who intend no harm, and certainly not towards people who are entirely innocent because they are far removed from the incidents of human sufferings. In a revolution, however, such acts of violence are inescapable. If we take as examples the two revolutions which are held up as models by revolutionaries, the French and the Russian, this conclusion is forced upon us. Such acts of murder may perhaps be justified on other grounds. The principles that sanction counterviolence will not do.

Second, a nation that, by virtue of its social order, imposes economic hardships on any group among its citizens, while this is clearly, from the moral standpoint, a despicable state of affairs, is not an appropriate target for counterviolence. This does not mean that its citizens should refrain from taking effective action to right social policy. It means only that they should not engage in the form of violence which may bring death to others as a means of changing the course of social events. In the course of its long history, the Jewish people has frequently been the victim of economic oppression. Its members could not own land, engage in farming, and hold certain professional positions. This people responded with patriotism, struggle, and diplomacy—but never with violence. The restrained reaction was not due to fear or timidity but to a tradition which rejected violence as a means of rectifying economic injustice.

IV

The second argument in support of violence in the process of revolution does not depend on the notion of "the enemy." It justifies turning any citizen—whether he is guilty or innocent of any crime—into a victim if the purpose of society will be served. This is implicit in the notion of a calculus. The only relevant circumstance that the revolutionary must take into account is the quantity of happiness and the extent of its distribution. If following the revolution, more happiness is available and for more of society's members, violence even against those who are innocent of society's evils is indicated.

This argument presupposes several doctrines. It assumes: (1) The life of a human being may be taken in the interest of social well-being. Society may literally *sacrifice* its members in its advance to the goal of human happiness. (2) It is possible to calculate the quantity of happiness available prior to the revolution and the increase in happiness that the revolution will bring in its wake. (3) It is possible to determine in advance that the action taken by revolutionaries will, at least with a high degree of probability, bring about the social order envisioned by them. These assumptions will be scrutinized.

1. It is true that, in the Jewish scheme of values, life does not occupy the highest position. For example, defending the Jewish community's right to live according to Torah is assigned greater value than the preservation of life. It is not only in the defense of the community against physical attack that one is required to

risk his life; the sacrifice of life is also an obligation when the spiritual life of the community is threatened. In the case of the individual, faith in the God of Israel is assigned similiar priority. If, for example, a Jew is given the option of idolatry or death, and there is no alternative, he is commanded to choose the latter.[9] In short, Judaism agrees that life may be subordinated to a social purpose. Indeed this is true of every society which, at the very least, assigns less importance to human life than to the preservation of the community and its defense against attack. Judaism differs, however, in its conception of the location of life in the scale of values. It does not subordinate life to the purpose of achieving a wider distribution of material, intellectual, and technological goods. In other words, it does not permit the sacrifice of life to the goal of happiness as happiness is construed by contemporary revolutionaries.

2. Is a calculus possible? Can we calculate the quantity of happiness in a prerevolutionary society, the cost of change, and the improvement in the quality of life postrevolution? There are several objections to the suggestion that it can be done. First, there is the value of life itself. How shall we quantify it? Lives will be sacrificed in the revolution. What number shall we assign to a life in the calculus?

Judaism's view is that it cannot be done. The equation suggested in the Talmud implies that a calculus in which human life is a variable is an impossible objective. In a passage which addresses itself to the question of the obligation to preserve the life of another, one learns, "He who preserves one life is credited with saving the entire world."[10] It is a peculiar equation: one life equals the life of society. This sort of equivalence renders quantification impossible. (Marcuse, in fact, grants this. He writes, "Who can quantify and who can compare the sacrifices exacted by an established society and those exacted by its subversion? Are ten thousand victims more ethical than twenty thousand?" His answer is that in absolute ethical terms, there is no justification for violence; but in a historical context, a calculus can be constructed out of materials which can be estimated, namely, resources and means of distribution. Does this mean that life has no value in the context of history, or is he saying that we must discard life as a variable because it is not calculable? Neither option is acceptable.)

But there are objections of a general philosophical sort. If happiness is a goal, it is relevant to ask, on what does happiness depend? The availability or possession of goods is only one factor. Are there not others—the sense of identification with a community, commitment to a cause, creativity, etc.—which cannot be included among distributable goods? But why should such factors not be included in the calculus? The power that resides in a quantified formula in physics derives from the fact that it is experimentally demonstrated that one factor depends only on one or two or three others and *on none besides*. If the calculus proposed is to have any merit at all, it must first be shown that happiness depends on the distribution of available goods and on *nothing else*.

Further, how shall equations in the calculus be formulated? Does happiness vary as the square of the value of bread? Is it linearly proportional to knowledge? Is it inversely proportional to the third power of pain? The tasks of measurement and quantification present insuperable problems. The notion of a calculus in the domain under discussion betrays either ignorance of scientific method or wishful thinking or both.

3. The most incomprehensible ingredient in the revolutionary's program is his belief that by means of violence he will be able to translate his vision into reality. It is possible to infer from cause to effect if scientific laws relating the two, invariably or statistically, are available. But I know of no laws in the social sciences which imply that the application of violence in a definite historical context will bring about definite results. There are no laws which can assure specific results even with a high degree of probability. The suggestion that revolutions have in fact produced desirable results (discussed earlier in the essay) is fallacious. Since, as has been noted, the element of social progress is an ingredient in the definition of revolution, no social upheaval has been called a revolution if it did not contribute to progress. But surely, the introduction of violence to effect social change has not always, or even in most instances, resulted in progress. The view that a better

society will be achieved by a program of violence turns out to be a pious hope.

V

Is violence the sole instrument of social change? Several points need be clarified. First, there are those who deny that violence is at all useful as an instrument of social progress. Two contradictory maxims are frequently heard, one from opponents and the other from supporters of violence. One reads, "violence breeds violence." The implication of this declaration is that violence cannot serve as a means to the revolutionary goal. The other maintains, "violence is the only way." Its advocates are always ready to cite examples of its accomplishments. In fact neither of these opposing claims is universally true. Violence can be used to annihilate the opposition, and if it is successful, as has sometimes been the case in the course of human history, the need for further violence is obviated. On the other hand, the results of violence are not always gratifying. There are instances of violence, intended to transform society, that ended in disaster. In any case it is never easy to trace the cause of a phenomenon in the social domain; and we are usually mistaken when, in a fluid and rapidly changing society, where many factors are constantly at work, we attempt to identify a single element as the cause of the social event.

Second, methods other than violence may be available which are to be preferred. Certainly Judaism thinks so. Those personalities in Jewish history who, more than any others, devoted themselves to the task of social change were the prophets. They were keenly sensitive to the prevailing corruption and exploitation in society. But the prophets, to a man, advocated methods other than violence. They employed preaching, teaching, exhortation, and demonstration to impress society's members with the need for commitment to moral principles in human relations. To effect this, they called for penitence—penitence rather than violence as an instrument of social progress. This expresses the essence of the Jewish view. At the very least, therefore, Judaism adheres to the conviction that methods other than violence *can* accomplish effectively a social transformation.

But the prophetic approach also implies a rejection of violence as a method of social change. I should like to propose a theoretic basis for this rejection. To begin with, a distinction should be made between the immediate and the ultimate goals of a revolutionary ideology. Generally such an ideology projects a vision of social possibility. The vision is distant, unreachable, at least at the moment, and in the category of a dream. It is an ultimate goal. If the ideology also introduces a program, it will include a method of attaining an immediate objective. In the ideology under consideration in this chapter, the ultimate goal is happiness; the immediate objective is the redistribution of available goods; the method is violence. It is conceivable that the method suggested for effectively achieving the immediate objective is inconsistent with the realization of the ultimate goal.

Now, the attainment of the ultimate in the social vision does not depend on the rearrangement of the social order and the restructuring of its institutions alone. It also requires the moral transformation of human personalities. What is needed is a method of molding individuals who respect the rights of others and who are responsive to their problems; in prophetic terms, men with capacities for justice and compassion. A society of such *humane* personalities cannot be achieved merely by changing social patterns. It will not do to argue that individual behavior reflects the character of society, for it is equally true that society mirrors the characteristics of its members. The relation between society and individual is an organic one—in the Kantian sense, that is, both are mutually cause and effect of each other.

Human transformations of a moral sort, however, cannot be achieved if the method of violence is endorsed as a legitimate revolutionary technique. Violence introduces insensitivity and cruelty into the human personality. This conclusion may best be exhibited by way of a comparison. Another method that those devoted to the cause of social progress employ is civil disobedience. It is sometimes suggested that violence is merely a step beyond civil disobedience and a natural outgrowth of it. This is not the case. The two are far apart and opposite in direction. One who engages in civil disobedience exposes only himself to harm; those who are violent are prepared to inflict death and injury on others. The former demonstrates, by the sacrifices that he makes, that his action is motivated by commitment to principle; the motivation of those who are violent is always suspect. One who is civilly disobedient influences by convincing; one who is violent compels by coercion. The endorsement of violence as a means of social change encourages, especially among the uncommitted and the opportunistic in society, callousness and brutality. Such a technique will clearly not produce the type of personality that can serve as a basis for the creation of a society that embodies in its patterns the ideals of justice and peace.

Hence, while violence may produce a world in which available goods are equally distributed, it is detrimental to the attainment of the ultimate goal of mankind.

VI

Judaism has always concerned itself with social change. Every religion that projects a vision of a better world, in the manner in which prophetic Judaism does, will always be critical of existing conditions. Those inspired by the spirit of Judaism will invariably work towards the transformation of the status quo so that it may approach in character the content of the vision. The realization of the ultimate, however, demands as an indispensable prerequisite moral inclinations that are inconsistent with the practice of violence.

Notes

1. Salo W. Baron, *A Social and Religious History of the Jews*, vol. 1 (New York: Columbia University Press, 1937), p. 22.

2. Bertrand Russell, in *Power* (New York: Norton, 1938), p. 35, defines power as the production of intended effects. The definition formulated here differs from Russell's in that he characterizes power in terms of its actual use, while the one offered here defines it in terms of potentiality. I believe that *power* has always been a term in the category of the potential rather than the actual.

3. *Novum Organum*, bk. I, aphorism 3.

4. This is the meaning of *work* as the term is employed in the commandment that prohibits work on the Sabbath Day. God created the realm of nature in six days and rested from the work of creation on the seventh. Man should refrain from similar work on the Sabbath.

5. Deuteronomy 8:12–14.

6. Ibid., 17:16–17.

7. See Bahya, *Hovot ha-levavot*, Sixth Treatise, chap. 8.

8. Deuteronomy 8:17.

9. See Francis Bacon's *The New Atlantis*.

10. *Utilitarianism* (New York: Liberal Arts Press, 1953), p. 39.

11. Deuteronomy 17:18–20.

12. *The Philosophy of Nietzsche* (New York: ModernLibrary, 1927), p. 419.

13. The fact that the element of commitment is regarded as a second component should not be taken to imply that it is totally independent of the first. It may be the case that Jewish culture, i.e., the Torah, has the capacity to inspire such commitment. It may be, however, that Jewish commitment arose out of other, perhaps historical, considerations.

14. It is useful to stress this because of the recent tendency in the scholarly segment of the Jewish community to forget the fact that, classically, the power of the book to the Jew means a commitment to Torah values rather than the power of logical analysis and knowledge. The contemporary intellectual quality

of the Jewish people did indeed emerge out of a commitment to study as prescribed by Torah, but an examination of the current Jewish intellectual scene does not reveal that commitment is one of its components.

15. Bavli, *Sanhedrin* 7b.

16. Bavli, *Makkot* 7a.

17. Bavli, *Sanhedrin* 71a.

18. *Yad, Hilkhot Sanhedrin* 14:10.

19. Bavli, *Sanhedrin* 74a.

20. See chap. 15.

21. "War and Nonresistance," in *Philosophy in the Age of Crisis*, ed. E. Kykendall (New York: Harper & Row, 1970), pp. 245–246.

22. Deuteronomy 17:15.

23. *Ethics of the Fathers* 6:2.

24. Bavli, *Berakhot* 7a.

25. *Ethics of the Fathers* 3:2.

26. *Yad, Hilkhot Melakhim* 11:4, 12:1–2.

27. Bavli, *Sanhedrin* 19a. In one instance, a sovereign had accumulated sufficient power to intimidate the court and the procedure was suspended.

28. I Samuel 8:5 and the commentaries of Rabbi David Kimḥi (Radak) and Rabbi Levi ben Gershon (Ralbag).

29. Isaiah 11:3–4.

CHAPTER 2

1. See the discussion of this question in M. R. Cohen, *Reason and Nature* (Glencoe: Free Press, 1931), pp. 401–412.

2. See John Rawls, *A Theory of Justice* (Cambridge: Harvard University Press, 1971), pp. 118 f.

3. According to Norman Podhoretz, this is, in effect, the result of the United Nations resolution that equated Zionism and racism. He writes, in "The Abandonment of Israel," *Commentary*, July 1976, p. 23, "It is necessary to bear in mind what this Zionism–racism resolution said about the state of Israel. The resolution did not merely condemn the state of Israel for alleged crimes against the Palestinians, or for discriminating against its own Arab citizens. What the resolution did was to denounce the state of Israel itself as an illegitimate entity. The very idea of a sovereign Jewish state in the Middle East (Zionism), let alone the actuality of one, no matter what its boundaries might be, was by definition declared criminal (racist). In the eyes of this resolution, Israel could only cease to be criminal if it ceased to be both Jewish and sovereign—if, in other words, it ceased to exist."

4. *The Zionist Idea*, ed. Arthur Hertzberg (New York: Meridian Books, 1960), p. 222.

5. *On Zion* (New York: Schocken Books, 1973), pp. xix–xx.

6. Ibid., p. xx.

7. Leviticus 25:16.

8. *Yad, Hilkhot Melakhim* 4:6.

9. *Yad, Hilkhot Issurei Bi'ah* 14:7.

10. Morris R. Cohen, *Reason and Law* (Glencoe: Free Press, 1950), p. 108.

11. *Bava Mezia* 32a.

12. *Sanhedrin* 6b.

13. While the possession of the holy land was a privilege conferred upon the Jews in the Covenant Between the Parts, it is also an obligation. See, for example, the fourth criticism of Naḥmanides of the positive commandments of Maimonides in the latter's *Sefer ha-Mitzvot*.

14. Maimonides, *Yad, Hilkhot Shabbat* 2:5.

15. For it is clear that, even when an individual is threatened with death in the event that he fails to violate a Jewish precept, his unwillingness to submit will not *necessarily* result in death. The one who pronounced the threat may not have intended to carry it out in the first place or he may relent. Such a situation, therefore, is one where death is *probable*, i.e., it occurs in most instances, but not necessarily.

16. *Bava Batra* 34a.

17. Ibid. 28a.

18. An ancient commentary cited in the *Shitah Mekubbezet* of Bezalel Ashkenazi on *Bava Batra* 34a.

19. Ibid., commentary of Rabbi Asher ben Yehiel (Rosh).

20. *Bava Batra* 41a.

21. *Yalkut*, Exodus 12:2.

22. *Yad, Hilkhot Beit ha-Beḥirah* 6:16 and *Hilkhot Terumot* 1:5.

CHAPTER 3

1. Exodus 20:12.

2. Deuteronomy 17:11.

3. This example of the Ḥanukkah lights is, according to Maimonides, a good illustration of the biblical precept cited here. Naḥmanides disagrees. See the debate in the first *shoresh* of the *Sefer ha-Mitzvot*.

4. Deuteronomy 17:15.

5. *Ḥovot ha-Levavot*, Sixth Treatise, chap. 8.

6. Among them is, for example, Rabbi Ẓevi Hirsch Chajes (known as the Maharatz Chajes). He is quoted by Menachem Elon, *Ha-Mishpat ha-Ivri* (Jerusalem: Magnes Press, 1973), vol. 1, p. 46, n. 143.

7. *Yad, Hilkhot Melakhim* 3:10.

8. R. Nissim b. Reuben Gerondi, *Derashot ha-Ran*, ed. Leon A. Feldman (Jerusalem: Institute Shalem, 1974), pp. 191–192.

9. *Sanhedrin* 48b–49a.

10. *Yad, Hilkhot Sanhedrin* 4:13.

11. Ibid. *Hilkhot Melakhim* 1:4.

12. Beit ha-Beḥirah on *Sanhedrin* (Frankfurt: Hermon Press), ed. A. Sofer, p. 212.

13. *Yad, Hilkhot Melakhim* 3:10.

14. Leviticus 25:10.

15. *Yad, Hilkhot Melakhim* 1:7.

16. *Sanhedrin* 20a.

17. *Mishpat Kohen* (Jerusalem, 1937), p. 337.

18. For a more complete discussion of this point, see below, chap. 11.

CHAPTER 4

1. Maimonides, *Yad, Hilkhot Genevah* 1:1.

2. Ibid., Hilkhot *De'ot* 6:3.

3. Numbers 27; Bavli, *Bava Batra* 115a.

4. Genesis 1:26.

5. Bavli, *Sanhedrin* 37a.

6. F. J. E. Woodbridge, ed., *Hobbes: Selections* (New York: Scribner's, 1930), p. 249.

7. John Rawls, *A Theory of Justice* (Cambridge: Harvard University Press, 1971), p. 508.

8. *Yad, Hilkhot Teshuvah* 5:2.

9. Bavli, *Berakhot* 17a.

10. *Yad, Hilkhot Genevah* 1:1.

11. Ibid., *Hilkhot Gezelah ve-Avedah* 5:13–14.

12. Sol Roth, "Two Concepts of Humility," *Tradition* 13, no. 4 and 14, no. 1 (1973):5.

13. Numbers 12:3.

14. *Ethics of the Fathers* 4:4.

15. There is an exception, however. We must distinguish between a sense of superiority that flows from personal achievement and one that is a consequence of group belonging. A Jew is not permitted to think that he is better than a non-Jew because of his personal successes, but he may experience a sense of superiority on the grounds that he is a member of the Jewish community, whose life is patterned by Torah, which does possess greater value.

16. Naḥmanides on Leviticus 19:18.

17. *Yad, Hilkhot De'ot* 6:3.

18. Yaakov Ẓevi Meklenburg, *Ha-Ketav ve-ha-Kabbalah* on Leviticus 19:18.

19. *Yad, Hilkhot Avel* 4:1.

20. *Kitvei ha-Ramban* (Jerusalem: Mosad Harav Kook, 1913), vol. I, p. 374.

CHAPTER 5

1. *Yad, Hilkhot Gezelah ve-Avedah* 5:14.

2. Bavli, *Bava Mezia* 30a.

3. For example, see Bavli, *Bava Kamma* 72b and *Sanhedrin* 27a, in which it is declared that a scoundrel, halakhically defined, is not acceptable as a witness.

4. *A Theory of Justice* (Cambridge: Harvard University Press, 1971), p. 60.

5. This formulation derives from Aristotle, *Politics*, bk. III, chap. 9. He writes, "Justice is thought . . . to be, and is, equality, not, however, for all, but only for equals. And inequality is thought to be, and is, justice: neither is this for all, but only for unequals."

6. Leviticus 25:36.

7. Bavli, *Ta'anit* 11a.

8. Bavli, *Shevu'ot* 39a.

9. For the distinction between the two love obligations, see the chapter entitled "The Love Imperative" in Sol Roth, *The Jewish Idea of Community* (New York: Yeshiva University Press, 1977), pp. 41–57.

10. Such universality is explicitly demanded by Maimonides in connection with theft, robbery, and murder. See *Yad, Hilkhot Gezelah ve-Avedah* 1:2, *Hilkhot Genevah* 1:1, *Hilkhot Roze'ah u-Shemirat Nefesh* 1:1.

It is noteworthy that a similar view is expressed by Meiri (quoted in *Shitah Mekubbezet* on *Bava Kama* 113a), who makes a distinction between religious personalities and idol-worshippers. He writes: "In regard to those whose actions conform to the requirements of religions . . . if they come before us in litigation, we do not deviate as much as the width of a needle but allow justice to pierce the mountain [i.e., to run its course] whether we judge in their favor or for their adversaries. . . . In the case of idolators and those who do not conform to the demands of religions, one is not permitted to steal from them . . . nor is he allowed, by deceit, to cancel a debt. However, one is not obligated to return to him an object that was lost . . . because returning such an object is an act of generosity [*middat hassidut*], as distinct from morality, which is not mandatory with respect to one who has no religion whatsoever."

While opinions on this matter are not uniform, Meiri and Maimonides are at one in regard to the moral obligations of the Jew towards every one in the human community—Jew, gentile, even idolator. Whether an individual is or is not a religious person, indeed, even if he lacks moral character, he is entitled to moral treatment by his fellow man. Justice, in its moral sense, allows no exception to its application.

11. This is one of the essential ingredients in Kant's exposition of the categorical imperative.

12. Leviticus 19:15.

13. Bavli, *Bava Kama* 113a.

CHAPTER 6

1. Cf. the commentary of Rashbam on Bavli, *Bava Batra* 54b.

2. Exodus 19:16–18.

3. *Shabbat* 88a.

4. *Eiruchin* 21a.

5. *Yad, Hilkhot Gerushin* 2:20.

6. *The Jewish Idea of Community* (New York: Yeshiva University Press 1977), chap. 5.

7. *Bava Batra* 47b; Maimonides, *Yad, Hilkhot Mekhirah* 10:1.

8. Rashbam on *Bava Batra* 47b.

9. Bavli, *Bava Batra* 54b.

10. Rashbam on *Bava Batra* 54b.

11. "The Lonely Man of Faith," in *Studies in Judaica*, ed. Leon D. Stitskin (New York: KTAV, 1974), p. 122, n. 18.

12. *Yoreh De'ah* 268:2.

13. *Megillah* 26a.

14. Cited in Menachem Elon, *ha-Mishpat ha-Ivri* (Jerusalem: Magnes Press, 1973), vol. II, p. 588.

15. Cf. ibid., p. 590; also Hatam Sofer, Responsa on *Hoshen Mishpat*, responsom 11b.

16. Cf. Elon, *Ha-Mishpat ha-Ivri*, pp. 585–587; Hatam Sofer, loc. cit.

17. *A Theory of Justice* (Cambridge: Harvard University Press, 1971), pp. 142–143.

CHAPTER 7

1. *Yad, Hilkhot Melakhim* 3:9.

2. "The Justification of Civil Disobedience," in Steven M. Cahn, ed., *A New Introduction to Philosophy* (New York: Harper & Row, 1971), p. 485.

3. See the quotation above.

4. Op. cit., p. 490.

5. Rashi on Genesis 37:2.

6. Deuteronomy 15:11. Even if, according to some rabbinic interpreters of this biblical passage, poverty can indeed be eliminated, its total absence is seen as contingent, not on improved social policy, but on religious conduct. See Rashi on ibid. 15:4.

7. Of course, it is possible for an individual to dissent on both contractual and covenantal grounds. He is a member of a democratic state which is founded on contractual principles and has, in addition, accepted a covenantal relation to the Supreme Being. He has not, in making a covenantal commitment, yielded his right to demand conformity to the terms of the social contract.

8. It should be noted that the debate with respect to American Jewish dissent against Israeli policies has focused more on the methods dissenters choose to employ than on the right itself. No participant in the debate, for example, has argued that the would-be dissenter may not go to Israel and express his disagreements to the heads of the Israeli government or to members of the Knesset.

CHAPTER 8

   1. Deuteronomy 12:8.
   2. Ibid. 17:11.
   3. *On Liberty* (Chicago: Gateway, 1955), p. 24.
   4. Ibid. p. 18.
   5. In Robert E. Dewey and James A. Gould, eds., *Freedom: Its History, Nature, and Varieties* (London: Macmillan, 1970), p. 89.
   6. Spinoza, *Ethics*, pt. I, def. 7, and pt. I, proposition 17, corollary 2. The italics are mine.
   7. *Ethics of the Fathers* 6:2.
   8. It is true that the fundamental grounds for the justification of individual moral decisions, according to the new morality, is the uniqueness of problematic moral situations. If situations are unique, general moral rules are inapplicable, objective moral standards are irrelevant, and the individual becomes the exclusive judge of his own actions. I believe, however, that the freedom of self-determination with its elevation in importance of the arbitrary will provides another theoretical base for this new and radical moral theory.
   9. Roderick M. Chisolm, *Theory of Knowledge* (Englewood Cliffs, N.J.: Prentice-Hall, 1966), p. 11.
   10. Note that I am not concerned here with the problem of the freedom of the will but with the possibility of morality to one who is compelled to lead the life of a slave.
   11. Cf. Herbert J. Muller, "Freedom as the Ability to Choose and Carry Out Purposes," in Dewey and Gould, *Freedom*, p. 75.
   12. Cf. Justice William O. Douglas, "The Dennis Case: Revolutionary Party Speeches Must Be Allowed," in Dewey and Gould, *Freedom*, p. 241.

CHAPTER 9

   1. John Stuart Mill, *On Liberty* (Chicago: Gateway, 1955), p. 6.
   2. Deuteronomy 12:8.
   3. See commentary of Rashi on the phrase, "Ye shall proclaim liberty throughout the land unto all the inhabitants thereof," in Leviticus 25:10.
   4. See, for example, Maimonides, *Yad, Hilkhot Yesodei ha-Torah* 5:3.
   5. Ibid., *Hilkhot Gezelah ve-Avedah* 5:7–8.
   6. G. W. F. Hegel, *Reason in History* (New York: Liberal Arts Press, 1953), 42.
   7. Ibid., p. 29.
   8. Maimonides, *Yad, Hilkhot Yesodei ha-Torah* 5:5.
   9. In the Jerusalem Talmud, towards the end of the eighth chapter of the tractate *Terumot*, explicit reference is made to a city which was threatened with annihilation if its citizens would not surrender one from among them, and it is indicated that they were not permitted to do so.
   10. Maimonides, *Yad, Hilkhot Yesodei ha-Torah* 5:5.

11. Bertrand Russell, *Mysticism and Logic* (New York: Doubleday Anchor Books, n.d.), p. 81.

12. *Sanhedrin* 37a. It is worth noting that there is another version in which the phrase "of a Jew" is omitted. The passage would then refer to every human being.

13. Genesis 12:2.

14. *Shevu'ot* 39a.

15. See commentary of Siftei Kohen (Shakh) on *Yoreh De'ah* 242:3. Rama, on the other hand, declares that a student may disagree with his teacher if he possesses demonstrative proof that his teacher is in error.

16. Ibid., par. 4.

17. Ibid. 240:2.

18. Maimonides, *Yad, Hilkhot Mamrim* 1:2.

19. Naḥmanides on Deuteronomy 17:11.

20. *Eruvin* 13b.

21. Friedrich Nietzsche, *The Philosophy of Nietzsche* (New York: Modern Library, 1927), pp. 627–628.

CHAPTER 10

1. Roderick M. Chisolm, *Theory of Knowledge* (Englewood Cliffs, N.J.: Prentice-Hall, 1966), p. 11. Reference to this passage was made above in chap. 8.

2. See chap. 8.

3. See David Sidorsky, "Contemporary Reinterpretations of the Concept of Human Rights," in *Essays on Human Rights*, ed. David Sidorsky (Philadelphia: Jewish Publication Society, 1979), pp. 99–100.

4. Sol Roth, *The Jewish Idea of Community* (New York: Yeshiva University Press, 1977), p. 81.

5. Leviticus 19:17.

6. Of the seven Noachide commandments, only four prescribe duties to our fellow men. Two are concerned with our relationship to God, and one is relevant to the animal kingdom. Since human rights are deduced from universal obligations to man, it follows that, on the Jewish view, there are four basic human rights. The seven commandments are enumerated, among other locations, in Maimonides, *Yad, Hilkhot Melakhim* 9:1.

7. Friedrich Engels, "Communism and History," in *Philosophic Problems*, ed. Mandelbaum et al. (New York: Macmillan, 1967), p. 498.

8. *Yad, Hilkhot Teshuvah* 5:1. While this passage deals with the freedom of the will, it is also relevant to the issue of political freedom in society. One cannot, on the Jewish view, claim a political right to do that which is morally wrong; one can claim only permission to do so.

CHAPTER 11

1. Maimonides, *Yad, Hilkhot Melakhim* 1:3.
2. Bavli, *Berakhot* 55b.
3. Cf. *Pithei Teshuvah* on *Hoshen Mishpat* 3:8.
4. *Hoshen Mishpat* 2:1.
5. This quotation from the Responsa of Raanach appears in Menachem Elon, *Ha-Mishpat ha-Ivri* (Jerusalem: Magnes Press, 1973), vol. II, p. 573, n. 70.
6. This quotation appears in ibid., p. 46.
7. Bavli, *Kiddushin* 41b.
8. Cf. *Mordekhai* on *Bava Kamma* 178.
9. *Yad, Hilkhot Melakhim* 1:4–5.
10. Bavli, *Sanhedrin* 20b.
11. *Hoshen Mishpat* 188:2.
12. *Yad, Hilkhot Shelubin ve-Shutafin* 1:3.
13. Rema, *Hoshen Mishpat* 232:28.
14. *Yad, Hilkhot Mamrim* 1:4.
15. From *Responsa of the Rosh,* chap. 6, par. 5.
16. Bavli, *Bava Mezia* 59b.
17. *Hinnukh,* mitzvah 78.
18. Bavli, *Horayot* 4b.
19. Mishnah, *Rosh ha-Shanah* 2:9. See also the exposition of this view in Bavli, *Rosh ha-Shanah* 25a–b.
20. Deuteronomy 17:11.

CHAPTER 12

1. Isaiah 11.
2. Zechariah 8:16.
3. *Sanhedrin* 6b.
4. *Hoshen Mishpat* 12:2.
5. Bavli, *Derekh Erez Zuta,* the concluding chapter on peace. This view is also expressed by a talmudic sage in *Sanhedrin* 6b, who declares that, in every case, it is desirable that a court apply strict judgment, rather than pursue the path of compromise.
6. Hobbes, *Selections* (New York: Scribner's, 1930), p. 270.
7. See Sol Roth, "The Morality of Revolution: A Jewish View," *Judaism* 20, no. 4 (Fall 1971).
8. See, among other locations in talmudic literature, the chapter on peace in *Derekh Erez Zuta.*

CHAPTER 13

1. *Bava Batra* 54b.

2. *Ethics of the Fathers 3:2.*

3. Cf. Sol Roth, "The Doctrine of Separation," in *The Jewish Idea of Community* (New York: Yeshiva University, 1977).

4. Deuteronomy 8:3.

5. Isaiah 50:6–7. While these verses appear to refer to the experiences of the prophet, the tribulations described, in the face of which the prophet stands firm, reflect the history and attitude of the Jewish people. The biography of the prophet and the history of the people are parallel. It is, therefore, with good reason that both are designated "The servant of God."

6. Jon Woocher, "Civil Judaism," a study of the National Jewish Resource Center.

7. *Ta'anit* 11a.

8. *Shevu'ot* 39a.

CHAPTER 14

1. *Sefer ha-Ḥinnukh*, mitzvah 20.

2. Bavli, *Sanhedrin* 17b.

3. Bavli, *Bava Kamma* 113a.

4. Maimonides, *Yad, Hilkhot Teshuvah* 5:2.

5. Yerushalmi, *Ḥagigah* 1:7.

CHAPTER 15

1. Hannah Arendt, *On Revolution* (New York: Viking, 1963), p. 21.

2. In *Philosophy in the Age of Crisis*, ed. Eleanor Keykendell (New York: Harper & Row, 1970).

3. *Sanhedrin* 72a.

4. This conclusion is based on the mishnah in *Oholoth* 7:7 and a passage in *Sanhedrin* 72b. It is also cited as law in Maimonides, *Yad, Hilkhot Roze'aḥ u-Shemirat Nefesh.* 1:9; and in Karo's *Ḥoshen Mishpat* 425:2.

Since the mishnah in *Oholot* has also been cited in connection with other halakhic problems, not relevant to our discussion, clarification is in order. The mishnah consists of two parts. The first deals with a fetus that threatens the mother's life. The mishnah authorizes the destruction of the fetus to save the mother. The second is concerned with a threat to the mother's life following the moment in the birth process at which the fetus legally acquires individuality. At this point, according to the mishnah, the infant's claim to life equals that of the mother. As the mishnah puts it, "One life may not be taken to save another." It is the second part that is relevant to our discussion. Counterviolence in the case of the infant (no longer a fetus following the legal fact of birth) is proscribed because the intention to do violence is lacking. Analogously, if an adult were unintentionally threatening the life of another, e.g., a man is accidentally falling from a height on a pedestrian, the latter may not preserve himself by deliberately killing the unwilling assailant. Thus Meiri, on the passage in *Sanhedrin* cited above, generalizes from the case of the infant, "Whenever the designation *rodef* does not apply, life may not be taken."

5. Meiri on *Sanhedrin* 72b.

6. *Sanhedrin* 74a.

7. Maimonides, *Yad, Hilkhot Genevah* 4:10–11.

8. Leviticus 19:16.

9. The relevant talmudic passages are in *Sanhedrin* 74a, "By a majority vote, it was resolved in the upper chambers of the house of Nithza in Lydda that in every other law of the Torah, if a man is commanded: 'Transgress and suffer not death; he may transgress and not suffer death, excepting idolatry, incest [which includes adultery], and murder.' But this holds only if the Jewish community is not under attack by a government intent on destroying its spiritual life. In the event that the community is threatened, one must submit even for a lesser principle. When R. Dimi came he said: 'This was taught only if there is no royal decree, but if there is a royal decree, one must incur martyrdom rather than transgress even a minor precept.' "

10. *Sanhedrin* 37a. This quotation is a translation of the passage in the Munich text.

Index

Agency, law of and democracy, 129-41
Akiva, R., and death penalty, 15; and democracy, 140; justice and dissent, 91
Alienation, and *Galut*, 152-64
Arendt, Hannah, 177
Attitudes, commitment to community, 2; and *Galut*, 152-64; individuals, rights and obligations, 107

Bacon, Francis, 8
Berlin, Isaiah, 95
Buber, Martin, 29-30

Citizenship, justice and consent, 72-82
Civil disobedience, justice and dissent, 83-92
Coercion, justice and consent, 72-82
Commitment: and cultural power, 14; equality and justice, universality of, 62-71; and *Galut*, 152-64; justice and consent, 72-82; obligation of individual, 104-16; state and power, 1
Community: equality and justice, 62-68; freedom, rights and powers, 93-103; and *Galut*, 152-64; human rights, 117-28; Jewish idea of, 1; justice and consent, 72-82; land use, 30-32; peace and justice, 142-51; role of individual in, 104-16; state and power, commitment to, 1; values of, 2
Compulsion, justice and consent, 72-82
The Concept of Liberty, 95
Covenants, land rights, 26-39

Creativity, of individuals, 104-16; use in creation of power, 9
Cultural distinctions, justice and equality, 62-71
Cultural power, 14-15

Death penalty, coercive power of state, 15-16
Destiny, common destiny of community, 2; and *Galut*, 152-64
Diaspora, and *Galut*, 152-64
Dissent, justice and dissent, 83-92
Dosa, R., and democracy, 140

Eliezer, R., and democracy, 138
Equality, 4; political equality and *Galut*, 152-64; rights and obligations under, 52-61
Estrangement, and *Galut*, 152-64
Ethical relations, equality, rights and obligations under, 57-61
Exile, *Galut*, 152-64

Freedom: component of justice, 4; concepts of, 93-103; justice and dissent, 83-92; power of state, 19-20

Gamaliel, R., and democracy, 140

Herzl, Theodore, 28
Hobbes, Thomas, 20; and peace, 147; sovereignty and divine will, 45
Holy Land, rights to land, 25-39
Humility: equality of man, 58-61; exercise of state power, 10

203